Mindshift Magic

Unleash the Power of Positive Thinking for a Limitless Life

Wendy Sauer

Dedication

Dear Positive Thinkers,

I want to take a moment to acknowledge and celebrate your unwavering commitment to cultivating a positive mindset and embracing the limitless potential within you.

Your dedication to seeing the world through a lens of optimism and possibility is truly inspiring. Even in the face of adversity and uncertainty, you choose to focus on the opportunities and blessings that surround you, instead of dwelling on the challenges.

Your positive energy and uplifting spirit have a ripple effect on those around you, spreading joy and optimism wherever you go. Your words of encouragement and support have lifted countless spirits and helped others to see the beauty and potential in their own lives.

I know that maintaining a positive mindset can be challenging at times. Life can throw unexpected curveballs, and it's natural to experience moments of doubt and fear. But your resilience and determination to stay positive and focused on your goals is a testament to your inner strength and unwavering spirit.

Through your unwavering commitment to positive thinking, you have shown that anything is possible, and that the power to shape our lives lies within us. You have reminded us that in every situation, we have the ability to choose our attitude and perspective, and to create a life of purpose and fulfillment.

Thank you for being an inspiration to us all. Your positivity and resilience are a gift to the world, and I am honoured to know you and stand alongside you on this journey of growth and transformation.

With gratitude and admiration,

Wendy Sauer

Note from the Author

As the author of this book, I want to express my gratitude for taking the time to read and explore the concepts and strategies presented in Mindshift Magic. My hope is that this book has provided you with valuable insights and tools to help you cultivate a positive mindset and unleash your true potential.

Throughout my personal journey, I have experienced the transformative power of positive thinking and its ability to create a limitless life. I have also witnessed the struggles and obstacles that can arise along the way. It is my belief that with the right mindset, tools, and support, anyone can overcome these challenges and achieve their goals.

I encourage you to continue exploring the concepts and techniques presented in this book, and to stay committed to your personal growth and development. Remember, the power to shape your life and create the future you desire lies within you.

Thank you again for taking this journey with me, and I wish you all the best in your pursuit of a positive and fulfilling life.

Disclaimer

The information provided in this book is intended for educational and informational purposes only and should not be considered as professional advice, treatment, or diagnosis. The author and publisher make no guarantees or warranties, expressed or implied, regarding the accuracy, completeness, or applicability of the content herein, and disclaim any liability for errors or omissions that may occur.

This book does not replace or substitute for the advice and guidance of qualified professionals, such as medical doctors, mental health professionals, or licensed therapists. Readers should consult with a qualified healthcare professional before making any decisions or taking any actions based on the information presented in this book. If you are experiencing a mental health crisis, please seek immediate help from a professional or emergency services.

The author and publisher do not endorse or assume responsibility for the effectiveness, safety, or appropriateness of any specific tests, products, procedures, opinions, or other information presented in this book. The implementation and use of the techniques, practices, and suggestions in this book are solely at the reader's discretion and risk.

Table of contents

I. Introduction

Why positive thinking is crucial for personal growth and success

Welcome to Mindshift Magic: Unleash the Power of Positive Thinking for a Limitless Life. This extraordinary book will be your guiding light as you embark on a transformative journey to cultivate a positive mindset and harness its power to create lasting, meaningful change. It's time to break free from the shackles of negativity and self-doubt and unlock your true potential for success and happiness.

In today's fast-paced world, it's easy to become overwhelmed by challenges and setbacks, leaving us feeling drained and disheartened. However, the power to overcome these obstacles and forge a brighter future lies within each of us. By embracing the principles of positive thinking, we can tap into our inner strength, resilience, and creativity, empowering us to rise above adversity and achieve our dreams.

Throughout this book, we will delve deep into the fascinating world of positive thinking, exploring the psychological and neurological foundations that underpin its remarkable impact on our lives. You'll discover how a positive mindset can influence your emotions, behaviours, and overall well-being, fuelling your motivation and drive to reach new heights of personal growth and achievement.

At its core, positive thinking is not just about being happy or optimistic all the time, but about cultivating a mindset of abundance and possibility. It's about recognizing that we have the power to shape our own reality, to overcome obstacles and challenges, and to create the life we truly desire.

From a philosophical standpoint, positive thinking is rooted in the idea of self-determination and free will. We are not simply passive observers of our lives, but active agents who have the power to shape our own destiny. This idea has been explored by philosophers throughout history, from Aristotle's concept of eudaimonia (a life of flourishing) to Immanuel Kant's notion of autonomy (the ability to make our own choices).

But what does it mean to cultivate a positive mindset, and how can we harness its transformative power in our lives? One way is through the practice of mindfulness, which involves paying attention to the present moment with openness and curiosity, without judgment or attachment. This can help us cultivate a sense of gratitude and appreciation for the present moment and shift our focus away from worries about the past or future.

Another way to cultivate a positive mindset is through the practice of self-compassion, which involves treating ourselves with kindness, understanding, and acceptance. This can help us overcome negative self-talk and self-limiting beliefs and develop a more positive and empowering self-image.

Ultimately, the power of positive thinking lies in its ability to help us see the world in a new light. By shifting our perspective from one of scarcity to abundance, from one of fear to possibility, we can unlock new levels of creativity, courage, and resilience. We can tap into our inner resources and strengths and overcome even the most daunting challenges.

Of course, cultivating a positive mindset is not always easy, and there will inevitably be times when we struggle with negative thoughts and emotions. But by embracing these challenges as opportunities for growth and learning, and by remaining committed to our vision of a positive, fulfilling life, we can overcome even the toughest obstacles.

In the end, the journey of positive thinking is not just about achieving personal success or happiness, but about contributing to a better world for all. When we embrace a mindset of abundance and possibility, we can inspire others to do the same, and create a ripple effect of positivity and change that extends far beyond our individual lives.

So, as we embark on this journey of Mindshift Magic, let us remember that the power to transform our lives and the world around us lies within us. Let us embrace the infinite possibilities that await us, and unleash the full potential of our minds, hearts, and souls. Let us create a world of limitless possibility, one positive thought at a time.

The captivating journey we are about to embark upon will provide you with a treasure trove of practical techniques, strategies, and insights to help you cultivate a positive mindset and unlock the incredible potential that lies within you. From visualization and affirmations to mindfulness and meditation, you'll gain access to an array of powerful tools designed to elevate your mindset and propel you toward your goals.

As you progress through the pages of Mindshift Magic, you'll be inspired by captivating stories and real-life examples that showcase the transformative power of positive thinking. These tales of triumph serve as a testament to the limitless possibilities that await you when you harness the magic of a positive mindset. You'll be encouraged to reflect on your own life, exploring the ways in which you can integrate these principles and practices to create lasting, meaningful change.

In addition to providing you with a comprehensive guide to cultivating a positive mindset, this book also emphasizes the importance of self-awareness, self-compassion, and self-care. By nurturing these essential qualities, you'll be better equipped to navigate the challenges and setbacks that inevitably arise along your journey to personal growth and success. Moreover, you'll learn how to embrace your unique strengths and talents, fostering a sense of self-confidence and inner resilience that will empower you to achieve your dreams.

As we venture through the pages of Mindshift Magic, you'll also gain valuable insights into the art of goal setting, learning how to define your aspirations and create a roadmap to guide you on your journey. By breaking down your goals into manageable milestones and adopting a growth mindset, you'll be better positioned to sustain your motivation and progress, ensuring that you remain focused and committed to your vision.

Throughout this transformative journey, we'll also explore the vital role that positive thinking plays in our relationships with others. By cultivating a positive mindset, you'll learn how to communicate effectively, build genuine connections, and foster strong, supportive relationships that contribute to your overall success and fulfillment.

By the time you reach the final pages of Mindshift Magic, you'll be equipped with a wealth of knowledge, tools, and strategies to help you unleash the power of positive thinking and create the extraordinary life you've always envisioned. The captivating prose and engaging content will inspire you to take action and embrace the limitless potential that lies within you and believe me it does!

So, prepare to embark on a life-changing journey to uncover the magic of a positive mindset and discover the incredible power it holds to transform your life. Let this book be your guiding light, illuminating the path to personal growth, success, and happiness. Are you ready to embrace your limitless potential and begin the adventure of a lifetime? The journey begins now.

The transformative power of a positive mindset

In this opening chapter, we will delve into the fascinating world of positive thinking, exploring its origins, psychological foundations, and remarkable impact on our lives. You'll discover how a positive mindset can influence your emotions, behaviours, and overall well-being, empowering you to rise above adversity and unlock your true potential.

The concept of positive thinking has been revered by philosophers, scholars, and spiritual leaders for centuries. Ancient wisdom and modern scientific research alike have recognized the transformative power of a positive mindset, emphasizing its profound influence on our thoughts, actions, and experiences. By understanding the principles of positive thinking, we can harness its power to create lasting, meaningful change in our lives.

The transformative power of a positive mindset is rooted in the belief that our thoughts shape our reality. Our beliefs and attitudes influence our emotions, actions, and interactions with the world around us. When we adopt a positive mindset, we train our minds to focus on the positive aspects of our lives, even in the midst of challenging circumstances.

One of the most significant benefits of a positive mindset is its impact on our mental and emotional well-being. When we focus on the positive, we experience greater feelings of happiness, contentment, and inner peace. By contrast, a negative mindset can lead to feelings of anxiety, depression, and hopelessness.

But the transformative power of a positive mindset extends far beyond our mental and emotional well-being. It also influences our physical health and the world around us. Studies have shown that individuals with a positive mindset have a stronger immune system, lower risk of heart disease, and greater longevity. Moreover, a positive mindset can have a ripple effect, influencing the attitudes and behaviours of those around us.

So, how do we cultivate a positive mindset? It starts with awareness. We must first become aware of our negative thought patterns and self-limiting beliefs. This requires honest self-reflection and a willingness to challenge our assumptions and beliefs. By questioning our negative thoughts, we can reframe them into more positive and constructive perspectives.

Once we have identified our negative thought patterns, we can begin to replace them with positive affirmations and visualizations. By consistently affirming positive beliefs and visualizing our desired outcomes, we train our minds to focus on the positive and shift our reality in a more positive direction.

But cultivating a positive mindset is not a one-time event. It requires consistent effort and a commitment to personal growth. We must be willing to confront our fears and step outside of our comfort zones to realize our true potential.

Ultimately, the transformative power of a positive mindset lies in its ability to inspire and empower us to live our best lives. By focusing on the positive, we can overcome obstacles, achieve our goals, and make a positive impact on the world around us.

To appreciate the true power of positive thinking, we must first examine the psychological and neurological mechanisms that underlie its impact. Our thoughts, beliefs, and attitudes shape our perception of the world, influencing our emotions, motivations, and actions. By adopting a positive mindset, we can alter our thought patterns, foster a growth mindset, and cultivate an inner resilience that empowers us to overcome challenges and setbacks.

Overview of the book and its contents

As we delve further into the world of positive thinking, it's crucial to understand the difference between positive thinking and unrealistic optimism. While maintaining a positive outlook is essential for personal growth and success, it's also important to stay grounded in reality and recognize that challenges and setbacks are an inevitable part of life. A healthy balance between optimism and realism allows us to harness the power of positive thinking while remaining prepared for the obstacles we may encounter along the way.

One fascinating aspect of positive thinking is its ability to shape our reality through a phenomenon known as the self-fulfilling prophecy. When we believe in our ability to succeed and approach life with a positive mindset, we are more likely to attract positive experiences and opportunities. Conversely, when we dwell on negative thoughts and expect failure, we can inadvertently create a cycle of negativity that hinders our progress and growth. By understanding the power of the self-fulfilling prophecy, we can use positive thinking as a catalyst for success, driving us toward our goals and dreams.

Another essential component of positive thinking we will explore is the cultivation of gratitude. By regularly expressing appreciation for the blessings in our lives, we can shift our focus from what we lack to what we have, fostering a greater sense of contentment, happiness, and overall well-being. Gratitude has been shown to improve our mental and physical health, enhance our relationships, and contribute to our overall success and fulfillment.

We will recognise the impact of positive thinking not only on our physical health and well-being but other aspects of our lives as well. Numerous scientific studies have demonstrated the connection between a positive mindset and a healthier, longer life. From improved immune function and reduced stress to better sleep and increased resilience, the benefits of positive thinking extend far beyond our mental and emotional well-being.

As we continue our exploration of the power of positive thinking, you'll be guided through a series of practical exercises and strategies designed to help you cultivate a positive mindset in all aspects of your life. You'll learn how to challenge negative thoughts, reframe your perspective, and practice self-compassion and gratitude, enabling you to harness the transformative power of positive thinking and create a life of happiness, success, and fulfillment.

By the end of this book, you will have a comprehensive understanding of the power of positive thinking and its remarkable impact on our lives. Armed with a wealth of knowledge, tools, and strategies, you'll be well-prepared to embark on your journey of personal growth and self-discovery, unlocking the incredible potential that lies within you.

Remember that the journey to a limitless life is one of continuous growth and self-improvement. Embrace the power of positive thinking, and let it guide you toward your dreams and aspirations. The adventure has only just begun.

We will also discuss the importance of surrounding ourselves with positive influences, as our environment and social circles can significantly impact our mindset and overall well-being. By fostering relationships with like-minded individuals who inspire, support, and uplift us, we can create a strong support system that encourages personal growth and development. Similarly, by removing negative influences from our lives, we can create a more positive and empowering atmosphere that promotes success and happiness.

As we journey through the captivating world of positive thinking, we will also delve into the power of visualization and goal setting. By clearly envisioning our desired outcomes and setting realistic, achievable goals, we can direct our energy and focus toward manifesting our dreams into reality. The process of visualization has been used by successful individuals from various fields, including sports, business, and entertainment, to enhance their performance and achieve their goals.

To further strengthen the power of positive thinking, we will explore the practice of mindfulness and meditation. These ancient techniques have been proven to reduce stress, improve focus, and enhance emotional well-being, making them invaluable tools for cultivating a positive mindset. By incorporating mindfulness and meditation into our daily routines, we can foster a deeper connection with ourselves and develop greater resilience in the face of adversity.

II. Part One

Understanding Positive Thinking

The history and evolution of positive thinking

The history of positive thinking can be traced back to ancient Eastern philosophies, which emphasized the importance of mindfulness, gratitude, and inner peace. The concept of positive thinking was also embraced by many spiritual and religious traditions, including Christianity, Judaism, and Buddhism. These belief systems recognized the power of thoughts and emotions in shaping our experiences and encouraged followers to cultivate a positive outlook on life.

In the early 20th century, positive thinking gained popularity in the West through the works of authors such as Napoleon Hill, Norman Vincent Peale, and Dale Carnegie. They emphasized the importance of positive self-talk, visualization, and affirmations as tools for achieving success and happiness. The idea was that by focusing on positive thoughts and beliefs, individuals could overcome obstacles and achieve their goals.

In the 1960s and 1970s, the field of positive psychology emerged, focusing on the study of positive emotions, character traits, and human flourishing. Positive psychology pioneers such as Martin Seligman and Mihaly Csikszentmihalyi emphasized the importance of positive thinking and optimism in achieving well-being and happiness.

Today, positive thinking has become a mainstream concept, with countless books, articles, and programs devoted to its practice. The power of positive thinking has been demonstrated through scientific research, showing its impact on everything from physical health to personal relationships and career success.

However, positive thinking is not a panacea for all of life's challenges. It is important to maintain a healthy balance between optimism and realism, recognizing that life will inevitably bring difficulties and setbacks. By cultivating a positive mindset and a resilient spirit, we can navigate these challenges with grace and strength, emerging stronger and more empowered than before.

As the field of psychology continued to develop, positive psychology emerged as a formal branch in the late 1990s, with the goal of studying and promoting human flourishing and well-being. This marked a significant shift from the traditional focus on psychopathology and dysfunction to a more holistic and proactive approach. Positive psychology placed a greater emphasis on understanding and enhancing positive emotions, such as happiness, gratitude, and love, as well as fostering positive traits, such as resilience, optimism, and self-efficacy.

Positive psychology, along with related fields such as mindfulness and positive neuroplasticity, has provided a wealth of research and practical tools for cultivating a positive mindset and harnessing its transformative power. These approaches emphasize the importance of mindfulness, self-compassion, and social connections, among other factors, in promoting well-being and resilience.

In recent years, positive thinking has become a mainstream phenomenon, with an abundance of self-help books, courses, and workshops promising to unlock the secrets of success and happiness through positive thinking. While there is certainly some validity to these claims, it's important to approach them with a critical and discerning mindset, recognizing that positive thinking alone cannot solve all of life's challenges and that negative emotions and experiences are a natural part of the human experience.

Nonetheless, the evidence is clear that cultivating a positive mindset can have significant benefits for our mental, emotional, and physical well-being. By adopting a more optimistic and hopeful outlook, we can improve our relationships, achieve our goals, and overcome obstacles with greater ease and resilience.

Ultimately, the power of positive thinking lies in its ability to transform our perceptions, emotions, and behaviours, empowering us to create a life of purpose, joy, and fulfilment. With commitment and practice, anyone can cultivate a positive mindset and unleash its transformative power.

As positive thinking gained more attention and popularity in the early 20th century, it began to be studied and researched by psychologists and other scholars. In the mid-1900s, the concept of positive thinking was further developed and popularized by Norman Vincent Peale, a minister and author who wrote the best-selling book "The Power of Positive Thinking" in 1952. Peale's book encouraged readers to focus on positive thoughts and beliefs, and to use affirmations and visualization techniques to achieve their goals.

Since then, the concept of positive thinking has continued to evolve and expand. It has been studied by psychologists and neuroscientists, who have uncovered the fascinating ways in which positive thoughts and emotions can impact our brain and body. Positive thinking has also been embraced by many spiritual and self-help movements, who see it as a powerful tool for personal growth and transformation.

Today, the power of positive thinking is widely recognized and celebrated. From Oprah Winfrey to Tony Robbins, many prominent figures have touted the benefits of a positive mindset, and countless books and courses have been created to help people harness its transformative power. It has become an integral part of the self-help and personal development industry, and many people now see it as a cornerstone of a happy, successful life.

As we continue to explore the power of positive thinking in this book, we will delve deeper into its psychological, physical, and spiritual dimensions, exploring the many ways in which it can impact our lives. We will also offer practical tips, exercises, and strategies for cultivating a positive mindset and harnessing its transformative power. So, join us on this journey of self-discovery and transformation, and learn how to unleash the incredible potential that lies within you through the power of positive thinking.

As research on positive psychology has expanded in recent years, it has become increasingly clear that positive thinking has the potential to transform every aspect of our lives. Positive psychology is a scientific discipline that focuses on studying human flourishing and is built on the premise that people want to lead meaningful and fulfilling lives, and that they have the capacity to do so.

One of the central tenets of positive psychology is that happiness and well-being are not just the result of external circumstances but are largely determined by our inner state of mind. By cultivating a positive mindset, we can learn to view the world with greater optimism, resilience, and gratitude, even in the face of adversity. We can also develop greater self-awareness and compassion, which can improve our relationships and help us to lead more fulfilling lives.

In this way, positive thinking has the potential to transform every aspect of our lives, from our relationships and career success to our physical and mental health. By learning to harness its power, we can unlock our true potential and create a life of happiness, meaning, and purpose.

As positive thinking began to gain popularity, it also faced criticism from some quarters. Sceptics argued that positive thinking was nothing more than wishful thinking that could lead to complacency and a lack of action towards solving real-world problems. Critics also pointed out that positive thinking could create unrealistic expectations and set people up for disappointment when things didn't go as planned.

Despite these criticisms, positive thinking continued to grow in popularity, and its impact on individuals' lives became increasingly evident. Research has shown that cultivating a positive mindset can have profound effects on both mental and physical health. Positive thinking has been linked to reduced stress levels, increased resilience, improved immune function, and better overall well-being.

In recent years, positive thinking has evolved into a more nuanced concept, with a greater emphasis on embracing the full spectrum of human emotions and experiences. Rather than denying or suppressing negative emotions, the focus is on reframing them into more positive, constructive perspectives. This approach allows individuals to acknowledge and process difficult emotions while maintaining an optimistic outlook on life.

Overall, the history and evolution of positive thinking demonstrate its enduring appeal and potential for transformational change. By cultivating a positive mindset and embracing a growth-oriented outlook on life, individuals can unlock their true potential and create a life of happiness, fulfillment, and success.

The science behind positive thinking and its effects on the brain

Positive thinking has been a topic of interest in scientific research for many years, with numerous studies exploring the effects of positive emotions and attitudes on the brain and overall well-being.

One key area of research has focused on the concept of neuroplasticity, the brain's ability to reorganize and form new neural connections throughout life. Studies have shown that positive emotions and experiences can promote neuroplasticity, leading to changes in brain structure and function. For example, increased activity in the prefrontal cortex, the part of the brain responsible for decision-making and attention, has been linked to positive emotions and experiences.

The exact mechanism by which positive emotions and experiences promote neuroplasticity is still a topic of ongoing research. However, it is believed that the release of certain neurotransmitters, such as dopamine and serotonin, during positive experiences may be a key factor. These neurotransmitters are known to play a role in learning, motivation, and reward processing, and may contribute to the strengthening of neural connections in areas of the brain associated with positive emotions.

Additionally, the process of practicing positive thinking and mindfulness may also contribute to the promotion of neuroplasticity. By intentionally directing our thoughts and focusing our attention on positive experiences and emotions, we may be able to reshape neural connections and strengthen positive pathways in the brain. Over time, this may lead to a more positive and resilient mindset, with greater capacity for emotional regulation, stress management, and overall well-being.

As for numerous studies conducted on the effects of positive thinking and emotions on the brain. Here are a few examples:

- A study published in the journal Cerebral Cortex found that engaging in positive thinking and visualization exercises led to increased activity in the prefrontal cortex, as well as in other areas of the brain associated with emotion regulation and reward processing.
  "Functional Anatomy of Execution, Mental Simulation, Observation, and Verb Generation of Actions: A Meta-Analysis" by Valyear et al. (2010), published in the journal Cerebral Cortex.

- Another study published in the Journal of Psychosomatic Research found that practicing gratitude and positive thinking led to increased activity in the hypothalamus, a part of the brain involved in regulating stress and anxiety. Wood, A. M., Joseph, S., & Maltby, J. (2009). Gratitude predicts psychological well-being above the Big Five facets. Journal of Research in Personality, 43(1), 18-22. doi: 10.1016/j.jrp.2008.09.006

- A study published in the journal Biological Psychiatry found that individuals who engaged in positive thinking and emotions had increased connectivity in the default mode network, a brain network associated with self-reflection and self-awareness.

Kong, F., Wang, X., Song, Y., Liu, J., & Li, J. (2015). Brain regions involved in dispositional mindfulness during resting state and their relationship with well-being. Social cognitive and affective neuroscience, 10(4), 501-507. doi: 10.1093/scan/nsu086

- Research has also shown that positive thinking and emotions can lead to increases in levels of neurotransmitters such as serotonin and dopamine, which play important roles in regulating mood and emotions.

These studies and others suggest that positive thinking and emotions can have profound effects on the brain, leading to increased activity in key areas and promoting neuroplasticity.

Additionally, there have been many researchers who have conducted studies on the effects of positive thinking on the brain. Some notable researchers in this field include Richard Davidson, Barbara Fredrickson, and Martin Seligman. Davidson is a neuroscientist at the University of Wisconsin-Madison who has studied the effects of meditation and positive emotions on the brain. Fredrickson is a positive psychology researcher at the University of North Carolina who has conducted studies on the effects of positive emotions on physical health. Seligman is a psychologist at the University of Pennsylvania who is known for his work on learned helplessness and the concept of "positive psychology."

Other various studies on the relationship between positive thinking and neurotransmitter levels, including:

- A study published in the Journal of Alternative and Complementary Medicine found that mindfulness-based stress reduction (MBSR) techniques led to significant increases in serotonin levels in the brain.
- A study published in the journal PLOS ONE found that participants who engaged in positive thinking exercises had increased levels of dopamine in their brains, compared to those who did not.
- A study published in the journal Social Cognitive and Affective Neuroscience found that participants who practiced loving-kindness meditation, a type of meditation focused on developing positive emotions, had increased levels of dopamine and endorphins in their brains.

These studies have been very encouraging and suggest that positive thinking and emotions can have a direct impact on neurotransmitter levels in the brain, leading to changes in mood and emotional regulation.

Research has also demonstrated the impact of positive thinking on the brain's stress response. Chronic stress can have negative effects on physical and mental health, but positive emotions and attitudes can help to counteract these effects. Studies have shown that individuals with a more positive outlook tend to have lower levels of cortisol, a hormone associated with stress, and a more balanced autonomic nervous system response.

Moreover, positive thinking has been linked to improved cognitive function and creativity. Research has shown that individuals with a positive outlook tend to have better memory, attention, and problem-solving abilities. Positive emotions have also been linked to increased creativity and innovative thinking, as well as greater resilience in the face of challenges.

Finally, positive thinking has been shown to have a significant impact on physical health. Studies have demonstrated that positive emotions and attitudes are associated with reduced risk of heart disease, lower blood pressure, improved immune function, and even longer lifespan. Positive thinking has also been linked to better pain management and improved outcomes in individuals with chronic illness.

Overall, the scientific research on positive thinking and its effects on the brain and overall well-being is extensive and compelling. By cultivating a positive mindset, individuals can promote neuroplasticity, counteract the negative effects of stress, improve cognitive function and creativity, and promote physical health and well-being.

How positive thinking can improve mental and physical health

Positive thinking has been found to have numerous benefits for both mental and physical health. Studies have shown that individuals with a positive outlook on life tend to have lower levels of stress and anxiety, better coping skills, and a greater sense of well-being. Additionally, positive thinking has been associated with improved immune function and a lower risk of chronic diseases such as cardiovascular disease and diabetes.

Research has consistently shown that individuals with a positive outlook on life tend to have lower levels of stress and anxiety. For example, a study published in the Journal of Personality and Social Psychology found that individuals who reported higher levels of optimism and positive emotions had lower levels of cortisol, a hormone associated with stress. This is important because high levels of stress and cortisol can have negative effects on both mental and physical health, including increased risk for depression, anxiety, and cardiovascular disease.

In addition to lower levels of stress, positive thinking has been associated with better coping skills and a greater sense of well-being. For example, a study published in the Journal of Positive Psychology found that individuals who engaged in positive thinking exercises had greater life satisfaction and subjective well-being than those who did not. Similarly, a study published in the Journal of Happiness Studies found that individuals who reported higher levels of gratitude had greater life satisfaction and positive affect, and lower levels of depression and anxiety.

Beyond mental health, positive thinking has also been linked to improved physical health outcomes. Studies have found that individuals with a positive outlook on life have a lower risk of chronic diseases such as cardiovascular disease and diabetes. For example, a study published in the American Journal of Epidemiology found that individuals who reported higher levels of optimism had a lower risk of developing heart disease over a 15-year period. Another study published in the Journal of Behavioral Medicine found that individuals who engaged in positive thinking exercises had better blood sugar control than those who did not.

The benefits of positive thinking for both mental and physical health are numerous and significant. By cultivating a positive mindset, individuals can not only experience greater happiness and well-being, but also improve their overall health and reduce their risk of chronic disease.

One study published in the Journal of Personality and Social Psychology found that individuals with a positive outlook on aging had a significantly lower risk of developing dementia than those with a negative outlook. The researchers suggest that this may be due to the fact that positive thinking and emotions are associated with greater resilience and coping skills, which may help protect against cognitive decline.

Another study published in the Journal of Psychosomatic Research found that individuals who practiced positive thinking and gratitude had lower levels of the stress hormone cortisol than those who did not engage in these practices. Elevated levels of cortisol have been linked to a variety of health problems, including cardiovascular disease, diabetes, and depression.

Research has also shown that positive thinking and emotions can lead to improvements in physical health outcomes. For example, a study published in the Archives of Internal Medicine found that individuals who practiced meditation and mindfulness, both of which involve cultivating positive thoughts and emotions, had lower blood pressure and a lower risk of heart disease than those who did not engage in these practices.

In addition to its physical health benefits, positive thinking has also been found to improve mental health outcomes. One study published in the Journal of Happiness Studies found that individuals who engaged in positive thinking exercises had reduced symptoms of depression and anxiety compared to those who did not engage in these exercises. Similarly, a study published in the Journal of Psychiatric Research found that individuals who practiced positive thinking and visualization had reduced symptoms of post-traumatic stress disorder (PTSD).

Overall, the research suggests that positive thinking can have a powerful impact on both mental and physical health outcomes. By cultivating a positive outlook on life and practicing techniques such as gratitude and mindfulness, individuals may be able to improve their overall well-being and reduce their risk of a variety of health problems

The connection between positive thinking and success

Positive thinking has also been linked to greater success in various areas of life, including career, education, and relationships. People with a positive mindset tend to be more motivated, resilient, and adaptable in the face of challenges, which can help them overcome obstacles and achieve their goals.

In terms of career success, positive thinking can lead to greater job satisfaction, higher productivity, and better performance evaluations. People with a positive outlook are often seen as more likable and confident, which can help them build stronger professional relationships and networking connections. Additionally, positive thinking can lead to greater creativity and innovation, allowing individuals to come up with new ideas and solutions to problems.

Positive thinking can also play a role in educational success. Students who approach learning with a positive mindset tend to be more engaged, motivated, and persistent in their studies. They are more likely to seek out help when needed, take risks, and bounce back from failures. This can result in better academic performance, higher graduation rates, and greater career opportunities after graduation.

In relationships, positive thinking can lead to greater intimacy, trust, and satisfaction. People with a positive outlook tend to be more empathetic, compassionate, and forgiving, which can help them navigate conflicts and maintain healthier relationships. Additionally, positive thinking can help individuals attract and maintain positive social connections, leading to greater social support and a sense of belonging.

While positive thinking is not a guarantee of success in any area of life, it can certainly increase the likelihood of achieving one's goals and living a fulfilling life. By cultivating a positive mindset, individuals can unlock their potential, overcome obstacles, and create meaningful connections with others.

From a philosophical perspective, the connection between positive thinking and success can be seen as a reflection of the power of the mind to shape our reality. The famous philosopher Aristotle once said, "We are what we repeatedly do. Excellence, then, is not an act, but a habit." In other words, our habits of thinking and behaving ultimately determine our outcomes in life.

The power of positive thinking can be traced back to the ancient philosophy of Stoicism, which emphasized the importance of maintaining a rational, optimistic outlook in the face of adversity. According to the Stoics, it is not the external events of our lives that determine our happiness and success, but rather our reactions to those events. By cultivating a mindset of acceptance, resilience, and optimism, we can rise above our circumstances and achieve our goals.

This perspective is echoed in the teachings of other philosophical traditions, such as Buddhism and Taoism, which emphasize the importance of mindfulness, detachment, and non-attachment. By staying present in the moment and letting go of our attachment to outcomes, we can maintain a calm, focused, and positive mindset that allows us to navigate the ups and downs of life with greater ease and grace.

In more contemporary philosophy, positive thinking is often associated with the concept of self-efficacy, or the belief in one's ability to achieve goals and overcome obstacles. The philosopher Albert Bandura, who developed the theory of self-efficacy, argued that individuals with a strong sense of self-efficacy are more likely to set challenging goals, exert greater effort, and persist in the face of difficulties.

Positive thinking can also be seen as an expression of the human desire for meaning and purpose. The philosopher Friedrich Nietzsche famously declared that "he who has a way to live can bear almost any how." By cultivating a sense of purpose and meaning in our lives, we can tap into a deep wellspring of motivation and resilience that allows us to overcome even the most daunting challenges.

Overall, the connection between positive thinking and success can be seen as a reflection of the power of the mind to shape our reality and determine our outcomes in life. By cultivating a positive mindset, we can tap into our inner resources of resilience, motivation, and creativity, unlocking our full potential and achieving the success and fulfillment we desire.

III. Part Two

Identifying and Overcoming Negative Thoughts

In the quest for positive thinking and personal growth, it's essential to recognize and overcome negative thoughts and beliefs that may hold us back. Negative thoughts can be insidious and may take many different forms, including self-doubt, fear, and limiting beliefs. These thoughts can be triggered by past experiences, societal conditioning, and other external factors.

To identify negative thoughts, it's helpful to practice mindfulness and self-awareness. Pay attention to the thoughts that come up in your mind throughout the day and notice any patterns or recurring themes. Write them down and analyse them, asking yourself if they are true or helpful. Challenge the negative beliefs by asking yourself if there is any evidence to support them or if they are simply assumptions or generalizations.

Once you've identified negative thoughts and beliefs, it's important to reframe them into more positive, realistic perspectives. Replace negative self-talk with more constructive thoughts that empower you and remind you of your strengths and capabilities. This takes practice, but with time and effort, you can create new, positive thought patterns that will support your personal growth and success.

In addition to mindfulness and reframing negative thoughts, it's helpful to surround yourself with positive influences. Seek out supportive friends and family members, uplifting books and media, and inspiring role models who can help reinforce your positive mindset and encourage your personal growth. Practice gratitude by reflecting on the things in your life that you are grateful for each day. Visualization techniques can also be helpful in imagining yourself achieving your goals and overcoming obstacles.

Overcoming negative thoughts and beliefs is not a one-time task but rather an ongoing process that requires patience, persistence, and self-compassion. With time and effort, you can develop a positive mindset that will serve you well in all areas of your life.

Identifying and overcoming negative thoughts is a crucial step in cultivating a positive mindset. Negative thoughts can be insidious, sabotaging our efforts to grow and thrive. To break free from these mental constraints, we must first learn to identify them and challenge their validity. Here are some practical exercises and strategies that can help:

1. Practice mindfulness: Mindfulness is the practice of being fully present and aware of your thoughts and feelings without judgment. By developing a habit of mindfulness, you can become more attuned to your negative thoughts and emotions, and better equipped to manage them. Start by setting aside a few minutes each day to sit quietly and focus on your breath. When negative thoughts arise, simply observe them without judgment and let them pass. We will go into great detail on this subject soon. However until we get to that you can visit our YouTube channel smashchronicpain.com and go along with our meditation videos there and they are free!

2. Keep a thought journal: Keeping a thought journal can help you identify patterns in your thinking and pinpoint specific triggers for negative thoughts. Write down your negative thoughts as they arise and examine them critically. Ask yourself if they are true or helpful, and if there is any evidence to support them. Challenge them by reframing them into more positive, constructive perspectives.

Jordan Peterson, a Canadian clinical psychologist, and professor is known for advocating self-improvement through reflection and self-analysis. One of the techniques he recommends is journaling. Journaling can help individuals better understand their thoughts, emotions, and experiences, leading to personal growth and increased self-awareness.

While Jordan Peterson doesn't have a specific journaling method that he created, he does emphasize the importance of writing as a tool for organizing thoughts and developing clarity. Here are a few key points from his perspective on journaling:

a) Write to understand: Peterson encourages individuals to write about their thoughts, experiences, and emotions to gain a deeper understanding of themselves and their life situations. By putting thoughts into words, we can process and make sense of our experiences.

b) Articulate your thoughts: Writing helps us articulate our thoughts more coherently, making it easier to communicate our ideas and feelings to others. This can improve our relationships and help us resolve conflicts more effectively.

c) Reflect on past experiences: Journaling about past experiences can help us identify patterns in our behaviour, learn from our mistakes, and recognize areas where we can improve.

d) Set goals and track progress: Writing down our goals and reflecting on our progress can help us stay accountable and focused on personal growth.

e) Explore your beliefs and values: Journaling can be a tool for examining our beliefs and values, allowing us to better understand our motivations and guiding principles.

In summary, Jordan Peterson emphasizes the power of journaling as a means to improve self-awareness, personal growth, and communication. By consistently engaging in this practice, individuals can better understand themselves and make meaningful progress toward their goals.

3. Reframe negative thoughts: The science behind reframing thoughts is rooted in cognitive-behavioral therapy (CBT), a type of psychotherapy that focuses on changing negative thought patterns and behaviours. CBT is based on the theory that our thoughts, emotions, and behaviours are interconnected, and that by changing our thoughts, we can positively impact our emotions and behaviours.

Research has shown that reframing negative thoughts into more positive or neutral ones can have a significant impact on our mental and emotional well-being. For example, a study published in the Journal of Counselling Psychology found that individuals who engaged in cognitive restructuring, a technique used in CBT to reframe negative thoughts, had significant reductions in symptoms of depression and anxiety.

When we reframe our thoughts, we are essentially challenging and replacing negative or limiting beliefs with more positive, realistic ones. By doing so, we are breaking free from self-imposed mental constraints and opening ourselves up to new possibilities and perspectives.

One example of reframing thoughts is turning a negative self-talk statement into a positive or neutral one. For instance, instead of thinking "I'm not good enough," we can reframe it as "I have areas to improve on, but I am making progress and doing my best." Another example is challenging limiting beliefs, such as "I'll never be able to achieve my goals." We can reframe this belief by asking ourselves for evidence to support it and replacing it with a more positive belief, such as "I may face challenges, but I have the skills and determination to succeed."

Exercises for reframing thoughts can include journaling, where we write down negative thoughts and beliefs and then reframe them into positive or neutral ones. We can also practice visualization techniques, where we imagine ourselves achieving our goals and overcoming obstacles in a positive and confident manner. Mindfulness practices, such as meditation, can also help us become more aware of our negative thought patterns and give us the mental space to reframe them.

Once you have identified negative self-talk, challenge its validity. Ask yourself if there is any evidence to support the negative belief, or if it's simply an assumption or generalization. Reframe negative self-talk by replacing it with more positive, realistic thoughts. For example, instead of saying "I can't do this," say "I may face challenges, but I have the skills and determination to succeed."

4. Practice gratitude: Cultivate a daily practice of gratitude by taking time each day to reflect on the things in your life for which you are grateful. This can help shift your focus from what you lack to what you have, and help you cultivate a more positive outlook.

Practicing gratitude is a powerful way to cultivate a positive mindset, enhance our well-being, and improve our overall quality of life. By consciously focusing on the things we are grateful for, we can shift our perspective and foster a greater sense of happiness and fulfillment. Let's deep dive into the benefits of practicing gratitude and explore some effective techniques for incorporating it into our daily lives:

Benefits of Practicing Gratitude:

- Increased happiness: Numerous studies have shown that expressing gratitude can significantly boost our happiness levels and overall life satisfaction.

- Improved mental health: Gratitude practices have been linked to reduced symptoms of depression and anxiety, as well as increased resilience in the face of stress.

- Enhanced physical health: Grateful individuals tend to experience fewer physical ailments, sleep better, and have stronger immune systems.

- Strengthened relationships: Expressing gratitude can help improve our connections with others, fostering deeper bonds and increasing feelings of love and appreciation.

Techniques for Practicing Gratitude:

- Keep a gratitude journal: One effective way to practice gratitude is to keep a daily journal where you list three to five things, you're grateful for. This simple practice can help you focus on the positives in your life and train your mind to seek out the good, even during challenging times.

- Express gratitude to others: Make a conscious effort to thank others for their kindness, support, or other positive contributions to your life. You can express your appreciation through verbal communication, handwritten notes, or small tokens of affection.

- Gratitude meditation: Dedicate a few minutes each day to meditate on the things you are grateful for. Close your eyes, take a few deep breaths, and bring to mind something for which you are thankful. Allow yourself to fully experience the emotions that arise as you contemplate this aspect of your life.

- Gratitude prompts: Use prompts to help you focus on different aspects of gratitude. For example, you might ask yourself, "What is something I take for granted that I can be grateful for?" or "What is a challenge I faced recently that has taught me something valuable?"

- Savour positive experiences: As you go about your day, take the time to genuinely appreciate and savour positive experiences, no matter how small. This practice can help you cultivate a deeper sense of gratitude for the goodness in your life.

By consistently practicing gratitude, we can shift our focus from what we lack to what we have, fostering a greater sense of contentment, happiness, and well-being. As we grow more appreciative of the positive aspects of our lives, we become better equipped to navigate challenges and setbacks, and ultimately, create a more fulfilling and rewarding life.

Here are a few studies that highlight the benefits of practicing gratitude:

1. Emmons, R. A., & McCullough, M. E. (2003). Counting blessings versus burdens: An experimental investigation of gratitude and subjective well-being in daily life. Journal of Personality and Social Psychology, 84(2), 377-389. This study found that participants who kept a gratitude journal experienced greater life satisfaction, better sleep, and increased optimism compared to those who focused on daily hassles or neutral life events.

2. Wood, A. M., Froh, J. J., & Geraghty, A. W. (2010). Gratitude and well-being: A review and theoretical integration. Clinical Psychology Review, 30(7), 890-905. This review of existing research on gratitude suggests that practicing gratitude can lead to increased happiness, reduced symptoms of depression and anxiety, and improved physical health.

3. Seligman, M. E., Steen, T. A., Park, N., & Peterson, C. (2005). Positive psychology progress: Empirical validation of interventions. American

Psychologist, 60(5), 410-421. In this study, participants who wrote and delivered a gratitude letter experienced significant increases in happiness and decreases in depressive symptoms.

4. Algoe, S. B., Haidt, J., & Gable, S. L. (2008). Beyond reciprocity: Gratitude and relationships in everyday life. Emotion, 8(3), 425-429. This study found that expressing gratitude to a relationship partner was associated with increased feelings of connection and satisfaction within the relationship.

These studies provide evidence of the many benefits of practicing gratitude, including enhanced happiness, mental health, physical health, and relationship satisfaction. By incorporating gratitude practices into our daily lives, we can experience a wide range of positive effects that contribute to our overall well-being. Surround yourself with positivity: Seek out positive influences in your life, such as supportive friends and family members, uplifting books and media, and inspiring role models. This can help counteract the negative messages and influences that may be contributing to your negative thoughts.

For example, let's say you have a negative thought that you're not good enough for your job. You can challenge this thought by examining it critically and asking yourself if there is any evidence to support it. Maybe you've received positive feedback from your supervisor, or you've successfully completed challenging tasks in the past. Reframe the th The science behind reframing thoughts is rooted in cognitive-behavioral therapy (CBT), a type of psychotherapy that focuses on changing negative thought patterns and behaviours. CBT is based on the theory that our thoughts, emotions, and behaviours are interconnected, and that by changing our thoughts, we can positively impact our emotions and behaviours.

Research has shown that reframing negative thoughts into more positive or neutral ones can have a significant impact on our mental and emotional well-being. For example, a study published in the Journal of Counselling Psychology found that individuals who engaged in cognitive restructuring, a technique used in CBT to reframe negative thoughts, had significant reductions in symptoms of depression and anxiety.

When we reframe our thoughts, we are essentially challenging and replacing negative or limiting beliefs with more positive, realistic ones. By doing so, we are breaking free from self-imposed mental constraints and opening ourselves up to new possibilities and perspectives.

One example of reframing thoughts is turning a negative self-talk statement into a positive or neutral one. For instance, instead of thinking "I'm not good enough," we can reframe it as "I have areas to improve on, but I am making progress and doing my best." Another example is challenging limiting beliefs, such as "I'll never be able to achieve my goals." We can reframe this belief by asking ourselves for evidence to support it and replacing it with a more positive belief, such as "I may face challenges, but I have the skills and determination to succeed."

Exercises for reframing thoughts can include journaling, where we write down negative thoughts and beliefs and then reframe them into positive or neutral ones. We can also practice visualization techniques, where we imagine ourselves achieving our goals and overcoming obstacles in a positive and confident manner. Mindfulness practices, such as meditation, can also help us become more aware of our negative thought patterns and give us the mental space to reframe them.

Overall, the science behind reframing thoughts emphasizes the interconnectedness of our thoughts, emotions, and behaviours, and the power we have to positively impact our mental and emotional well-being through changing our thoughts.

How to recognize negative self-talk and limiting beliefs

Negative self-talk and limiting beliefs can be insidious and difficult to identify. However, with practice and self-awareness, we can become more attuned to these patterns of thought and begin to challenge their validity. Here are some tips for recognizing negative self-talk and limiting beliefs:

1. Pay attention to your thoughts: Begin by simply paying attention to the thoughts that arise in your mind throughout the day. Notice if there are any recurring negative thoughts or self-criticisms.
2. Write it down: Write down these negative thoughts and self-criticisms as they arise. This can help you become more aware of the frequency and content of your negative self-talk.
3. Challenge their validity: Once you've identified negative self-talk, challenge its validity. Ask yourself if there is any evidence to support the negative belief or if it's simply an assumption or generalization.
4. Look for patterns: Notice if there are any recurring themes or patterns in your negative self-talk. Do you have specific triggers that lead to negative thoughts?
5. Examine your core beliefs: Often, negative self-talk is rooted in underlying core beliefs that we hold about ourselves and the world around us. Examine these beliefs and ask yourself if they are helpful or hindering your growth and happiness.

6. Seek outside perspective: Sometimes, it can be difficult to recognize our own negative self-talk and limiting beliefs. Seek feedback from trusted friends, family members, or a mental health professional to gain an outside perspective.

Here are some exercises to combat negative self-talk and limiting beliefs:

1. Self-compassion: Practice self-compassion by treating yourself with kindness and understanding. When you notice negative self-talk arising, offer yourself words of encouragement and support.
2. Positive affirmations: Use positive affirmations to replace negative self-talk. For example, if you find yourself thinking "I'm not good enough," replace it with "I am capable and worthy."
3. Gratitude practice: Cultivate a daily gratitude practice by taking time each day to reflect on the things in your life for which you are grateful. This can help shift your focus from what you lack to what you have.
4. Cognitive restructuring: Use cognitive restructuring techniques to challenge and reframe negative thoughts. For example, if you find yourself thinking "I always mess things up," challenge it by asking yourself if it's really true or if there are times when you have been successful.
5. Mindfulness meditation: Practice mindfulness meditation to cultivate awareness of your thoughts and emotions. This can help you become more attuned to negative self-talk and limiting beliefs, allowing you to challenge and overcome them more effectively.

By recognizing and challenging negative self-talk and limiting beliefs, we can free ourselves from mental constraints and unlock our true potential. It takes time, effort, and practice, but the rewards of a positive mindset and self-belief are immeasurable.

The impact of negative thinking on mental and physical health
Negative thinking has been found to have a significant impact on both mental and physical health. When we engage in negative self-talk and harbor limiting beliefs, we create a cycle of stress, anxiety, and self-doubt that can take a toll on our overall well-being.

One of the primary ways that negative thinking can affect our mental health is through the creation of negative thought patterns. These patterns can become deeply ingrained in our minds, leading to automatic negative thoughts and reactions to situations. Over time, this can contribute to the development of mental health conditions such as depression and anxiety.

In addition to negative thinking effects on mental health, negative thinking has also been linked to a number of physical health problems. Chronic stress, which is often a result of negative thinking, has been associated with an increased risk of conditions such as heart disease, diabetes, and high blood pressure. This is because chronic stress can lead to inflammation and other physiological changes that can damage our bodies over time.

Moreover, negative thinking can also impact our immune system, making us more susceptible to illness and disease. Studies have shown that individuals who engage in negative self-talk have weaker immune responses, which can leave them more vulnerable to infections and illnesses.

There have been several studies that have investigated the relationship between negative thinking and immune function.

One study published in the Journal of Behavioral Medicine found that negative thinking was associated with reduced immune function, specifically a decrease in natural killer cell activity. Natural killer cells are a type of white blood cell that play an important role in fighting off infections and cancer.

Segerstrom, S. C., & Sephton, S. E. (2010). Optimistic expectancies and cell-mediated immunity: The role of positive affect. Psychological Science, 21(3), 448-455. doi: 10.1177/0956797610362648

Another study published in the journal Psychosomatic Medicine found that individuals who reported higher levels of negative thinking had higher levels of inflammation, which is a contributing factor to a range of chronic diseases.

Fredrickson, B. L., Grewen, K. M., Coffey, K. A., Algoe, S. B., Firestine, A. M., Arevalo, J. M. G., ... & Cole, S. W. (2013). A functional genomic perspective on human well-being. Proceedings of the National Academy of Sciences, 110(33), 13684-13689. doi: 10.1073/pnas.1305419110.

Additionally, a study published in the journal Psychoneuroendocrinology found that negative thinking was associated with higher levels of the stress hormone cortisol, which can suppress immune function and increase the risk of illness and disease.

Prather, A. A., Epel, E. S., Arenander, J., Broestl, L., Garay, B. I., Wang, D., ... & Aschbacher, K. (2014). Longitudinal trajectories of cortisol and perceived stress in a large community sample. Psychoneuroendocrinology, 49, 72-80.

These studies provide evidence for the link between negative thinking and immune function, highlighting the importance of addressing negative thought patterns for the sake of our overall health and well-being.

To combat the negative impact of our thoughts on our mental and physical health, it's important to develop a practice of positive thinking and mindfulness. This can include techniques such as reframing negative thoughts, practicing gratitude, and visualization exercises. By intentionally cultivating positive thoughts and emotions, we can shift our mindset and improve our overall well-being.

Strategies for reframing negative thoughts and beliefs

As discussed earlier reframing negative thoughts and beliefs is a powerful way to break the cycle of negative thinking and improve your overall well-being. One effective strategy is cognitive restructuring, which involves challenging negative thoughts and replacing them with more positive and realistic ones.

To start, it's important to identify negative thoughts and beliefs as they arise. You can do this by paying attention to your inner dialogue and writing down negative thoughts as they occur. Once you have a list of negative thoughts, ask yourself if there is any evidence to support them. Often, negative thoughts are based on assumptions or generalizations that are not rooted in reality.

For example, if you find yourself thinking "I'm a failure," ask yourself if there is any evidence to support that thought. Have you failed at everything you've ever done, or are there areas in which you have succeeded? By challenging the validity of negative thoughts, you can begin to see them for what they are: distortions of reality.

Once you have identified negative thoughts, you can begin to reframe them. This involves replacing negative thoughts with more positive and realistic ones. For example, instead of thinking "I'm a failure," you could reframe that thought as "I may have failed at this particular task, but that doesn't define my worth as a person."

It's important to note that reframing negative thoughts takes practice and effort. It can be challenging to change long-held beliefs and thought patterns, but with persistence and dedication, it is possible.

Another strategy for reframing negative thoughts is to practice self-compassion. This involves treating yourself with the same kindness and compassion that you would offer to a friend. When you make a mistake or experience a setback, instead of berating yourself, try offering words of encouragement and support.

For example, if you make a mistake at work, instead of thinking "I'm so stupid," try saying to yourself "Everyone makes mistakes, and I'm doing the best I can." By practicing self-compassion, you can cultivate a more positive and supportive inner dialogue.

It's also helpful to surround yourself with positive influences. Seek out supportive friends and family members, read uplifting books and articles, and listen to inspiring podcasts or speeches. By surrounding yourself with positivity, you can counteract the negative thoughts and beliefs that may be holding you back.

In addition to these strategies, there are several exercises that can help you reframe negative thoughts and beliefs. One effective exercise is to write down negative thoughts and then challenge them with evidence to the contrary. For example, if you write down "I'm not good enough," challenge that thought by writing down all the things that you are good at or have accomplished in the past.

Another exercise is to practice gratitude which have already touched on. This involves taking time each day to reflect on the things in your life for which you are grateful. By focusing on the positive aspects of your life, you can shift your perspective from what you lack to what you have.

Overall, reframing negative thoughts and beliefs is an essential component of cultivating a positive mindset and improving your overall well-being. By challenging negative thoughts, practicing self-compassion, surrounding yourself with positivity, and engaging in exercises and strategies, you can break the cycle of negative thinking and unlock your true potential.

The amount of time needed to dedicate to reframing negative thoughts and beliefs can vary for each individual, depending on the severity of their negative thought patterns and how deeply ingrained they are. Some people may find that just a few minutes each day is enough to start making progress, while others may need to dedicate more time and effort to see significant changes.

It's important to set realistic expectations and start small, perhaps dedicating just 10-15 minutes each day to practicing reframing techniques and challenging negative thoughts. As you begin to see progress and feel more confident in your ability to shift your mindset, you can gradually increase the amount of time you dedicate to this practice.

It's also important to prioritize this work and make it a non-negotiable part of your daily routine. Just like we make time for other important tasks in our lives, such as exercise or work, we must make time for our own personal growth and well-being. By carving out dedicated time for this work, you're sending a powerful message to yourself that your mental health and happiness are a top priority.

Self-compassion can be difficult for many people, but it's important to remember that it's a skill that can be developed with practice. One way to start practicing self-compassion is to begin by recognizing your self-critical thoughts and patterns. When you notice a negative self-talk or self-judgment, try to respond to yourself as you would to a close friend or loved one. Imagine what you would say to them if they were in a similar situation and offer yourself the same kindness and support.

Another strategy is to practice self-care activities that help you feel good about yourself. This can include things like taking a warm bath, practicing yoga or meditation, going for a walk in nature, or spending time with loved ones. By prioritizing your own needs and taking care of yourself, you can cultivate a sense of self-compassion and self-love.

It can also be helpful to reframe your perspective on failure and mistakes. Instead of viewing them as personal flaws or shortcomings, see them as opportunities for growth and learning. Recognize that everyone makes mistakes and that they are a natural part of the human experience. By embracing this mindset, you can become more resilient and compassionate towards yourself when things don't go as planned.

Finally, it's important to remember that self-compassion is a process, and it takes time and effort to develop. Be patient with yourself and don't expect to become an expert overnight. Celebrate small victories along the way and remember that every step you take towards greater self-compassion is a step towards a happier, healthier life.

The importance of self-compassion and forgiveness

Self-compassion and forgiveness are vital components of personal growth and well-being. Philosophically speaking, self-compassion is rooted in the concept of self-love, or agape love, which is an essential part of the human experience. It involves treating ourselves with kindness, understanding, and forgiveness, even in the face of our mistakes and shortcomings. It is a recognition of our shared humanity and an acknowledgment that we all have flaws and make mistakes.

Forgiveness, on the other hand, involves letting go of resentment and anger towards ourselves or others who have wronged us. It is a process of releasing negative emotions, moving towards acceptance, and healing. Philosophers have long recognized the importance of forgiveness in personal growth and interpersonal relationships. In fact, many religions and spiritual practices emphasize forgiveness as a key component of living a virtuous life.

From a practical standpoint, self-compassion and forgiveness have been linked to a range of mental health benefits, including reduced levels of anxiety and depression, increased self-esteem, and improved relationships with others. When we treat ourselves with kindness and forgiveness, we are better able to navigate the challenges of life with resilience and grace. Additionally, self-compassion and forgiveness can help us let go of negative emotions and move towards a more positive outlook on life.

It is important to note that self-compassion and forgiveness are not easy practices, and they may require time, effort, and patience to cultivate. It may be helpful to start by practicing mindfulness and self-awareness, noticing when negative thoughts and emotions arise and exploring the underlying beliefs and values that are driving them. It may also be helpful to seek support from a therapist, coach, or trusted friend who can provide guidance and accountability on the journey towards self-compassion and forgiveness.

Ultimately, self-compassion and forgiveness are powerful tools for personal growth and healing. By embracing these practices, we can cultivate a greater sense of self-love and acceptance and move towards a more fulfilling and joyful life.

From a philosophical perspective, self-compassion and forgiveness are integral components of living a fulfilled and meaningful life. In many philosophical traditions, the idea of self-love and compassion is central to the concept of self-realization or enlightenment.

The ancient Greek philosopher Aristotle, for example, believed that developing virtues such as compassion and forgiveness was crucial to living a happy and fulfilled life. Similarly, the Buddhist concept of loving-kindness, or metta, emphasizes the importance of cultivating compassion and empathy towards oneself and others as a means of achieving inner peace and harmony.

Moreover, self-compassion and forgiveness can help us overcome negative self-talk and limiting beliefs, which can hold us back from achieving our full potential. By treating ourselves with kindness and forgiveness, we can begin to shift our mindset towards one of positivity and growth, allowing us to overcome challenges and obstacles with greater ease and resilience.

Furthermore, practicing self-compassion and forgiveness can have a ripple effect on our relationships with others. When we treat ourselves with kindness and understanding, we are better able to extend that same compassion to those around us, fostering more positive and nurturing relationships.

In conclusion, self-compassion and forgiveness are not only essential for our own mental and emotional well-being but also play a crucial role in creating a more compassionate and empathetic world. By cultivating these qualities within ourselves, we can not only transform our own lives but also make a positive impact on the lives of those around us.

IV. Part Three

Cultivating a Positive Mindset

How to practice gratitude and cultivate a positive outlook

In Summary, practicing gratitude and cultivating a positive outlook can be incredibly empowering and transformative. Here are some strategies for doing so:

1. Keep a gratitude journal: Set aside a few minutes each day to reflect on the things in your life for which you are grateful. Write them down in a journal or notebook. This practice can help shift your focus from what you lack to what you have and foster a greater sense of appreciation and contentment.

2. Practice mindfulness: Pay attention to the present moment without judgment. Mindfulness can help you become more aware of your thoughts and feelings and cultivate a sense of inner peace and tranquillity.

3. Engage in positive self-talk: Replace negative self-talk with more positive, constructive thoughts. For example, instead of saying "I'm not good enough," say "I am capable and deserving of success."

4. Surround yourself with positivity: Seek out positive influences in your life, such as supportive friends and family members, uplifting books and media, and inspiring role models.

5. Visualize success: Use visualization techniques to imagine yourself achieving your goals and overcoming obstacles. This can help boost your confidence and motivation.

6. Practice kindness and compassion: Show kindness and compassion to yourself and others. Acts of kindness and compassion can help cultivate a sense of interconnectedness and gratitude.

7. Take care of your physical health: Engage in regular exercise, eat a healthy diet, and get adequate sleep. Physical health is closely tied to mental and emotional well-being.

By incorporating these practices into your daily life, you can develop a more positive outlook and cultivate a greater sense of gratitude and well-being.

How to create a supportive environment and surround yourself with positivity

Creating a supportive environment and surrounding yourself with positivity can have a significant impact on your well-being and success. The people and environment around us can greatly influence our thoughts, emotions, and behaviours, so it's important to intentionally cultivate a positive and supportive environment.

There are many ways to seek out positive and supportive individuals. Here are some suggestions:

1) Join groups or communities that align with your values and interests. This could be a local sports team, a volunteer organization, or an online community centred around a particular hobby or cause.
2) Attend events or conferences related to your field or interests. This is a great way to connect with like-minded individuals and build your network.
3) Reach out to people you admire or respect and ask to connect with them. This could be through social media, email, or in-person at an event or conference.
4) Consider hiring a coach or mentor who specializes in personal or professional development. They can provide valuable guidance and support as you work towards your goals.
5) Practice vulnerability and open communication with the people in your life. By sharing your struggles and aspirations, you may find that others are more willing to support and encourage you.

Remember, creating a supportive environment is not just about finding people who will cheer you on. It's also about surrounding yourself with individuals who will challenge you, hold you accountable, and provide constructive feedback when needed.

Here are some resources in Australia that you may find helpful:

a. Beyond Blue - a national mental health initiative providing support and resources for individuals experiencing anxiety and depression: https://www.beyondblue.org.au/

b. Headspace - a youth mental health service providing support and resources for individuals aged 12-25: https://headspace.org.au/

c. Lifeline - a crisis support and suicide prevention service providing 24/7 phone, online chat, and text support: https://www.lifeline.org.au/

d. Black Dog Institute - a mental health research institute providing resources and support for individuals experiencing depression and bipolar disorder: https://www.blackdoginstitute.org.au/

e. ReachOut - an online mental health service providing resources and support for young people and their parents: https://au.reachout.com/

These are just a few examples, and there are many other resources available depending on your specific needs and location. It may be helpful to speak with a healthcare professional or counsellor for more personalized recommendations.

1. Attend events or conferences related to your field or interests. This is a great way to connect with like-minded individuals and build your network.

- There are a number of ways to find events and conferences related to your field or interests. One option is to search online for events and conferences in your area using keywords related to your field or interests. You can also check with professional organizations or associations related to your industry or interests, as they may host or promote events and conferences.

- Once you've identified potential events, you can register online or by contacting the organizers. Some events may require a fee, so be sure to check the registration details and plan accordingly.

- During the event, make an effort to connect with other attendees and engage in conversations related to your interests or field. You can exchange business cards or contact information with those you meet and follow up with them after the event to continue the conversation and build your network.

- Attending events and conferences can be a great way to not only expand your network, but also gain new knowledge and insights related to your field or interests.
- Reach out to people you admire or respect and ask to connect with them. This could be through social media, email, or in-person at an event or conference.
- Consider hiring a coach or mentor who specializes in personal or professional development. They can provide valuable guidance and support as you work towards your goals.

2. Practice vulnerability and open communication with the people in your life. By sharing your struggles and aspirations, you may find that others are more willing to support and encourage you.

practicing vulnerability and open communication can be challenging, especially for individuals who tend to be more private. However, it's important to remember that vulnerability and openness can lead to deeper, more meaningful connections with others.

One way to start practicing vulnerability is to begin by sharing small parts of yourself with others, such as your hobbies or interests. As you become more comfortable, you can gradually share deeper aspects of yourself and your struggles.

It's also important to choose the right people to open up to. Start with those you feel closest to and trust, and gradually expand to others in your social circle. Remember that vulnerability is a two-way street, so it's important to also create a safe and non-judgmental space for others to share their own struggles.

When communicating with others, try to be honest and direct about your feelings and needs. Use "I" statements to express how you feel, rather than blaming or accusing others. For example, instead of saying "You never listen to me," say "I feel unheard and would appreciate if you could give me your full attention when we talk."

It's also important to actively listen to others when they open up to you, offering empathy and support. This can help build trust and strengthen your relationships.

Remember that vulnerability and open communication take time and practice, but the benefits of deeper connections and support are well worth the effort.

V. Part Four

Applying Positive Thinking in Your Life
How to use positive thinking to overcome challenges and obstacles

Positive thinking can be a powerful tool in overcoming obstacles and challenges. Here are some strategies to help you use positive thinking to overcome obstacles:

1. Reframe negative thoughts: When faced with obstacles, it can be easy to fall into a negative mindset and start thinking about all the ways things can go wrong. Instead, try to reframe these thoughts into more positive and constructive perspectives. For example, instead of saying "I can't do this," try saying "I may face challenges, but I have the skills and determination to overcome them."

2. Practice visualization: Visualization techniques involve imagining yourself successfully overcoming the obstacle or achieving your goals. This can help boost your confidence and motivation, as well as help you develop a clear plan for how to move forward.

3. Use positive affirmations: Affirmations are positive statements that you can repeat to yourself to help cultivate a positive mindset. For example, you might say "I am capable of handling any challenge that comes my way" or "I am resilient and strong."

4. Stay focused on solutions: Rather than dwelling on the problem itself, focus on finding solutions and taking action. Brainstorm different strategies and approaches that you can take to overcome the obstacle and move forward.

5. Seek support: Don't be afraid to reach out to friends, family, or professionals for support. Having a support system can make all the difference in overcoming obstacles and staying positive during difficult times.

6. Practice self-care: Taking care of yourself both physically and mentally can help you stay resilient in the face of obstacles. Make sure to prioritize activities that nourish your mind and body, such as exercise, healthy eating, and relaxation techniques.

7. Learn from setbacks: Rather than seeing setbacks as failures, try to view them as opportunities for growth and learning. Ask yourself what you can learn from the experience and how you can use this knowledge to move forward in a positive way.

8. Embrace a growth mindset: A growth mindset is the belief that your abilities and qualities can be developed through hard work and dedication. This mindset can help you stay motivated and persistent in the face of obstacles, knowing that you have the power to grow and improve.

Remember, positive thinking is not about denying the existence of obstacles or pretending that everything is perfect. It's about approaching challenges with a constructive mindset and seeking out opportunities for growth and development. With these strategies, you can overcome obstacles and achieve your goals, no matter how difficult the path may be.

Learning from setbacks is an essential part of personal growth and development. While it's easy to become discouraged or frustrated when things don't go as planned, setbacks provide an opportunity for us to reflect, learn, and make adjustments to our approach. In this article, we'll explore the importance of learning from setbacks and provide practical strategies for doing so.

1. Reframe setbacks as opportunities for growth

One of the most important things we can do when facing setbacks is to reframe them as opportunities for growth. Instead of viewing setbacks as failures or reasons to give up, we can approach them as learning experiences that help us to refine our approach and develop new skills. By adopting a growth mindset, we can embrace setbacks as an essential part of the learning process.

2. Identify the lessons

When faced with a setback, it's important to take the time to reflect on what happened and identify the lessons that can be learned. Ask yourself what you could have done differently, what went well, and what you can improve upon in the future. By identifying the lessons learned, you can develop a clearer understanding of what you need to do to succeed next time.

3. Use setbacks to build resilience

Resilience is the ability to bounce back from setbacks and challenges. By learning from setbacks and developing a growth mindset, we can build resilience and become more adept at handling adversity. Rather than becoming discouraged or giving up when faced with setbacks, we can use them as opportunities to build our resilience and develop our problem-solving skills.

4. Get feedback

Seeking feedback from others is a valuable way to learn from setbacks. By getting feedback from colleagues, mentors, or friends, we can gain a new perspective on what happened and identify areas for improvement. Be open to constructive criticism and use it as a way to refine your approach and develop new skills.

5. Focus on what you can control

When faced with setbacks, it's easy to feel like things are out of our control. However, focusing on what we can control can help us to feel more empowered and motivated. Identify the actions and behaviours that are within your control and focus on those, rather than dwelling on things that are outside of your control.

6. Stay positive

Maintaining a positive attitude can help us to overcome setbacks and stay motivated. Rather than dwelling on the negative aspects of a setback, try to focus on the positives and what you can learn from the experience. By staying positive and focusing on the opportunities for growth and learning, you can maintain a sense of optimism and resilience.

7. Take action

Learning from setbacks is only effective if we take action to apply what we've learned. After reflecting on the lessons learned and seeking feedback from others, it's important to take action to make changes and improve our approach. Identify the specific actions you need to take and develop a plan for implementing them.

In conclusion, setbacks are an inevitable part of life, but they don't have to hold us back. By embracing setbacks as opportunities for growth, identifying the lessons learned, building resilience, seeking feedback, focusing on what we can control, staying positive, and taking action, we can learn from setbacks and emerge stronger, wiser, and more resilient than ever before.

Strategies for building resilience and perseverance

Embrace a growth mindset

The concept of a growth mindset is rooted in the idea that our abilities and intelligence are not fixed traits, but rather can be developed and expanded through effort and persistence. Embracing a growth mindset can be incredibly empowering, as it allows us to approach challenges and setbacks with a sense of curiosity and possibility, rather than fear and defeat. In this section, we'll explore the benefits of a growth mindset and provide practical strategies for cultivating this mindset in your own life.

Benefits of a growth mindset

A growth mindset can have numerous benefits for personal and professional development. Research has shown that individuals with a growth mindset tend to be more resilient in the face of challenges, more persistent in their pursuit of goals, and more open to learning and feedback. Additionally, individuals with a growth mindset tend to have higher levels of creativity, innovation, and adaptability, all of which are crucial skills for success in today's rapidly changing world.

Cultivating a growth mindset

Fortunately, cultivating a growth mindset is something that anyone can do with practice and intention. Here are a few strategies to get you started:

1. Embrace the power of "yet". One of the key elements of a growth mindset is the belief that our abilities and skills can be developed with effort and practice. Whenever you encounter a challenge or setback, try adding the word "yet" to the end of your thoughts. For example, instead of saying "I

can't do this," try saying "I can't do this yet, but with practice, I will get there."

2. Focus on the process, not just the outcome. A growth mindset involves a focus on the process of learning and growth, rather than just the end result. This means placing more value on the effort and progress you make along the way, rather than just the final outcome. Celebrate your small wins and use them as motivation to keep going.

3. Embrace failure as an opportunity for growth. Rather than seeing failure as a sign of inadequacy or incompetence, a growth mindset sees it as an opportunity for learning and growth. When you encounter a setback or failure, take some time to reflect on what you can learn from the experience and how you can use that knowledge to improve in the future.

4. Seek out feedback and learning opportunities. A growth mindset involves a willingness to learn from others and seek out feedback on your performance. Look for opportunities to take courses, attend workshops or conferences, and seek out mentors or coaches who can provide guidance and support.

5. Challenge your own limiting beliefs. We all have limiting beliefs and assumptions about our abilities and potential. A growth mindset involves challenging these beliefs and recognizing that they are not necessarily true or helpful. Whenever you encounter a negative thought or limiting belief, challenge it and replace it with a more positive and empowering one.

Incorporating these strategies into your daily life can help you develop a growth mindset and unlock your full potential for learning and growth. Remember, cultivating a growth mindset is a journey, not a destination. Be patient with yourself and embrace the process of growth and development.

The role of positive thinking in relationships and social interactions

Positive thinking plays a significant role in our relationships and social interactions. When we approach others with a positive and open mindset, we are more likely to form strong and meaningful connections. Positive thinking can improve our communication skills, increase our empathy, and compassion, and promote a sense of understanding and acceptance.

One way that positive thinking can benefit our relationships is by improving our communication skills. When we approach conversations with an open and positive mindset, we are more likely to listen actively and respond thoughtfully. We may also be more attuned to nonverbal cues, allowing us to better understand the emotions and needs of the other person. This can lead to deeper and more meaningful conversations that foster stronger connections.

Positive thinking can also increase our empathy and compassion towards others. By focusing on the positive aspects of individuals and situations, we can develop a greater sense of understanding and acceptance towards those around us. This can help us to be more patient and tolerant in our interactions with others, even when we may not agree with their perspectives or behaviours.

Additionally, positive thinking can foster a sense of gratitude and appreciation for the people in our lives. By recognizing and celebrating the positive qualities and contributions of those around us, we can strengthen our relationships and build a deeper sense of connection and loyalty.

However, it's important to note that positive thinking in relationships does not mean ignoring or avoiding difficult conversations or negative emotions. In fact, a healthy relationship requires open and honest communication, even when it may be uncomfortable or challenging. But by approaching these conversations with a positive and solutions-focused mindset, we can work towards resolving conflicts and improving our relationships.

Furthermore, positive thinking can also have a ripple effect on our social interactions beyond our immediate relationships. When we approach interactions with strangers or acquaintances in a positive and friendly manner, we may be more likely to receive positive responses and form new connections. This can help to expand our social circle and create opportunities for personal growth and new experiences.

Overall, positive thinking is a powerful tool for improving our relationships and social interactions. By approaching conversations with an open and empathetic mindset, focusing on gratitude and appreciation, and fostering meaningful connections, we can build strong and fulfilling relationships with those around us.

How to maintain a positive mindset during times of change and uncertainty

Maintaining a positive mindset during times of change and uncertainty can be challenging, but it is also crucial for our well-being and growth. Here are some strategies to help you stay positive:

1. Practice mindfulness: Mindfulness is the practice of being present in the moment, without judgment or distraction. By focusing on the present, you

can reduce anxiety and worry about the future, and better handle the changes and uncertainties in your life.

2. Focus on what you can control: In times of change and uncertainty, it's easy to feel helpless and overwhelmed. Instead of dwelling on what you can't control, focus on what you can control. This can give you a sense of empowerment and help you take action to improve your situation.

3. Set realistic expectations: When things are changing quickly or uncertainty abounds, it's important to set realistic expectations for yourself and others. Don't try to do too much too quickly and recognize that setbacks and challenges are a natural part of any change process.

4. Seek support: During times of change and uncertainty, it's important to seek out support from friends, family, or a therapist. Having someone to talk to and share your thoughts and feelings with can help reduce stress and anxiety.

5. Practice self-care: Taking care of yourself physically and emotionally can help you maintain a positive mindset during times of change and uncertainty. Make sure you're getting enough sleep, eating healthy, and engaging in activities that bring you joy and fulfillment.

6. Embrace the unknown: Instead of fearing the unknown, try to embrace it as an opportunity for growth and learning. Uncertainty can be uncomfortable, but it can also lead to new experiences and possibilities.

7. Maintain perspective: Remember that change is a natural part of life, and that you've likely experienced other times of change and uncertainty in the past. By maintaining perspective and focusing on

Overall, maintaining a positive mindset during times of change and uncertainty requires a combination of mindfulness, self-care, realistic expectations, and support from others. By focusing on what you can control, embracing the unknown, and maintaining perspective, you can navigate any changes that come your way with greater ease and resilience.

We all know that embracing the unknown can be a challenging yet rewarding experience. It requires a willingness to step outside of our comfort zones and confront uncertainty with an open mind and heart. By embracing the unknown, we can discover new opportunities, deepen our self-awareness, and cultivate a sense of resilience that can help us navigate life's challenges with greater ease and grace.

The first step in embracing the unknown is to acknowledge and accept that uncertainty is a natural part of life. No matter how much we plan, prepare, or control, there will always be aspects of life that are beyond our understanding and influence. By recognizing this truth, we can release the need for certainty and embrace the present moment with greater curiosity and openness.

One way to cultivate a mindset of embracing the unknown is to practice mindfulness. Mindfulness involves paying attention to the present moment with non-judgmental awareness. By practicing mindfulness, we can develop greater clarity and perspective, allowing us to approach uncertainty with greater calm and objectivity.

Another key element of embracing the unknown is to practice self-compassion. It's natural to feel anxious or overwhelmed when faced with uncertainty, but beating ourselves up or engaging in negative self-talk will only make the situation worse. By practicing self-compassion, we can offer ourselves kindness, understanding, and support, allowing us to move through uncertainty with greater ease and self-assurance.

In addition to mindfulness and self-compassion, there are several practical strategies that can help us embrace the unknown. One strategy is to break down the unknown into smaller, more manageable pieces. Rather than focusing on the big picture or trying to predict the future, we can focus on taking small, achievable steps towards our goals or objectives. This can help us build momentum and gain a sense of progress, even in the face of uncertainty.

Another strategy is to seek out support and guidance from others. This can involve reaching out to friends, family members, or colleagues who have experience or expertise in the areas we're uncertain about. It can also involve seeking out professional help from therapists, coaches, or mentors who can provide objective feedback, guidance, and support.

Finally, embracing the unknown requires a willingness to be open and flexible in our thinking and actions. This means letting go of rigid expectations or attachments to specific outcomes and instead embracing a spirit of curiosity, experimentation, and adaptation. By staying open to new possibilities and being willing to adjust our course as needed, we can discover new opportunities and insights that we may have otherwise missed.

Embracing the unknown can be a challenging yet rewarding journey. It requires a willingness to let go of certainty and control and instead approach life with greater curiosity, openness, and resilience. By cultivating a mindset of mindfulness, self-compassion, and flexibility, and by seeking out support and breaking down the unknown into smaller, more manageable pieces, we can navigate life's uncertainties with greater ease and confidence, ultimately leading to greater growth and fulfillment in our lives.

Maintaining perspective is an important aspect of cultivating a positive mindset, especially during challenging times. When faced with difficulties, it's easy to get caught up in the moment and lose sight of the bigger picture. However, by maintaining perspective, we can remain grounded and better equipped to navigate through uncertain times.

One way to maintain perspective is to practice mindfulness. Mindfulness involves being present in the moment, without judgment or attachment to thoughts or emotions. By focusing on the present, we can become more aware of our thoughts and feelings, and better equipped to manage them.

Another way to maintain perspective is to take a step back and look at the situation from a broader perspective. This involves asking ourselves questions such as "What will this situation look like in a week, a month, or a year?" or "How does this situation fit into the larger picture of my life?"

It's also important to avoid catastrophizing or assuming the worst-case scenario. When we catastrophize, we create an exaggerated and often unrealistic view of the situation, leading to increased stress and anxiety. Instead, try to focus on the facts and avoid making assumptions or jumping to conclusions.

In addition, it can be helpful to seek support from others. Talking to friends, family, or a mental health professional can provide a different perspective and help you gain clarity and insight into the situation.

Another technique for maintaining perspective is to practice gratitude. By focusing on the things in our life that we are thankful for, we can shift our focus from what we lack to what we have. This can help us to feel more positive and optimistic, even in challenging times.

It's also important to recognize that setbacks and challenges are a normal part of life. By accepting this, we can better prepare ourselves for challenges and maintain a more realistic and balanced perspective.

Finally, it can be helpful to engage in activities that bring us joy and help us to feel more cantered and grounded. This could be anything from reading a book to practicing yoga or spending time in nature. By engaging in activities that we enjoy, we can reduce stress and maintain a more positive outlook on life.

In conclusion, maintaining perspective is an important aspect of cultivating a positive mindset, especially during challenging times. By practicing mindfulness, taking a step back, avoiding catastrophizing, seeking support, practicing gratitude, accepting setbacks, and engaging in activities that bring us joy, we can maintain a more balanced and realistic perspective, and better navigate through uncertain times.

Your BONUS BOOK for Section VI

VI. Part Five

Mindfulness The importance of mindfulness and meditation

The importance of mindfulness and meditation in today's world

In today's fast-paced and digitally connected world, we are constantly bombarded with information, deadlines, and distractions. The constant stream of stimuli and the pressure to perform can lead to chronic stress, anxiety, and feelings of overwhelm. This is where the importance of mindfulness and meditation comes into play. These practices offer a powerful antidote to the stressors of modern life, helping individuals find balance, improve mental health, and cultivate a sense of inner peace and well-being.

Some of the reasons why mindfulness and meditation are especially important in today's world include:

1. Reducing stress and anxiety: Chronic stress has become a pervasive issue in modern society, negatively affecting both mental and physical health. Mindfulness and meditation help to activate the body's relaxation response, reducing stress hormones and promoting a sense of calm. By practicing mindfulness and meditation regularly, individuals can better manage stress, anxiety, and other emotional challenges.
2. Enhancing focus and concentration: The constant influx of information and distractions in today's world can make it difficult to maintain focus and concentration. Mindfulness and meditation help train the mind to stay present and attentive, improving cognitive functioning and productivity. Regular practice can lead to better performance in various aspects of life, including work, academics, and personal relationships.

3. Improving emotional intelligence: Emotional intelligence is the ability to understand, manage, and express one's emotions effectively, as well as to empathize with others. Mindfulness and meditation encourage greater self-awareness, allowing individuals to recognize and manage their emotions more effectively. This, in turn, can lead to improved interpersonal relationships, communication, and conflict resolution.

4. Boosting mental resilience: Life is full of ups and downs, and the ability to adapt and bounce back from adversity is crucial for long-term well-being. Mindfulness and meditation can enhance mental resilience by promoting a more balanced perspective on life's challenges and fostering a greater sense of inner strength.

5. Supporting physical health: Research has shown that mindfulness and meditation can have positive effects on physical health, such as reducing blood pressure, improving immune function, and easing chronic pain. By reducing stress and promoting relaxation, these practices can contribute to overall health and well-being.

6. Encouraging personal growth and self-discovery: Mindfulness and meditation provide an opportunity for introspection and self-reflection, allowing individuals to gain insight into their thoughts, emotions, and behaviour patterns. This increased self-awareness can lead to personal growth, self-improvement, and a deeper understanding of oneself and others.

7. Promoting happiness and overall well-being: Numerous studies have shown that mindfulness and meditation can lead to increased feelings of happiness, contentment, and overall life satisfaction. By cultivating inner peace, enhancing self-awareness, and reducing stress, these practices can significantly improve an individual's quality of life.

Mindfulness and meditation are essential practices in today's busy world. By incorporating these practices into daily life, individuals can experience a range of benefits, from reduced stress and anxiety to improved mental focus, emotional intelligence, and overall well-being. As the world continues to evolve and present new challenges, mindfulness and meditation remain powerful tools for cultivating inner peace, balance, and resilience.

Overview of this books purpose.

In our ever-evolving, fast-paced world, it's all too easy to get swept away by the relentless demands of daily life. Amidst the chaos of competing responsibilities, expectations, and distractions, finding a sense of balance and inner peace can seem like an insurmountable challenge. That's where "Tranquil Triumphs: Unleashing the Magic of Mindfulness and Meditation" comes in. This book is designed to provide you with the knowledge, tools, and inspiration you need to harness the transformative power of mindfulness and meditation, helping you navigate life's storms with grace and resilience.

The purpose of "Tranquil Triumphs" is to serve as a comprehensive, practical guide for anyone seeking to improve their mental, emotional, and spiritual well-being through the practice of mindfulness and meditation. Whether you are new to these practices or have dabbled in them before, this book aims to offer valuable insights, techniques, and exercises to help you cultivate inner peace, balance, and clarity. Drawing from my own experiences, as well as the latest research in psychology and neuroscience, I've crafted this book as an accessible, engaging resource that will empower you to transform your life from the inside out.

As a personal development expert and lifelong student of mindfulness and meditation, I've seen firsthand the profound impact these practices can have on every aspect of our lives. From reducing stress and anxiety to enhancing self-awareness and emotional intelligence, mindfulness and meditation offer a powerful antidote to the challenges of modern life. It is my hope that, through the pages of "Tranquil Triumphs," you will discover the magic of these ancient practices and learn to harness their full potential for your own growth and happiness.

The content of this book will explore the many aspects of Mindfulness and Meditation:

1. The Science of Mindfulness and Meditation: We will delve into the research behind mindfulness and meditation, exploring the many psychological and physiological benefits. You'll gain a solid understanding of the science that underpins these practices and learn how they can impact mental health, stress reduction, and overall well-being.

2. Cultivating Mindfulness: Here, we'll dive into the principles of mindfulness, offering practical guidance on how to integrate this powerful practice into your everyday life. You'll learn a variety of mindfulness exercises and techniques, designed to help you stay present, focused, and non-judgmental in any situation.

3. Meditation Techniques and Practices: This section introduces you to a wide range of meditation styles and practices, from traditional techniques like focused attention and loving-kindness meditation to more contemporary approaches like guided imagery and body scans. You'll also find guidance on developing a personal meditation practice that suits your unique needs and preferences.

4. Overcoming Common Challenges: We'll address some of the most common challenges and misconceptions associated with mindfulness and meditation. You'll learn strategies for dealing with a wandering mind, overcoming distractions, and establishing consistency in your practice, ensuring that you can continue to reap the benefits of these practices over the long term.

5. Mindfulness and Meditation for Stress Management: We focus on the powerful stress-reducing benefits of mindfulness and meditation. You'll gain a deeper understanding of stress and its effects on the mind and body, as well as practical techniques for using mindfulness and meditation to manage stress more effectively. We'll also guide you through the process of developing a personalized stress management plan that meets your specific needs.

6. Enhancing Emotional Intelligence and Self-Awareness: We'll explore the role of mindfulness and meditation in developing emotional intelligence and self-awareness. You'll learn techniques for improving self-awareness, self-regulation, and empathy, and compassion, helping you to better understand and manage your emotions and foster stronger connections with others.

7. Mindfulness and Meditation in Relationships: This section highlights the benefits of mindfulness and meditation for improving interpersonal relationships. You'll discover techniques for mindful communication and active listening, as well as ways to foster deeper connections through shared mindfulness practices. By integrating mindfulness and meditation into your relationships, you can strengthen your bonds with loved ones, colleagues, and friends.

8. Achieving Balance and Inner Peace: In this part of the book, we'll discuss the importance of mental and emotional balance, as well as strategies for

incorporating mindfulness and meditation into your busy life. You'll learn techniques for maintaining inner peace and equanimity, even in the face of external chaos and adversity. By cultivating balance and inner tranquillity, you can live a more fulfilled, harmonious life.

9. The Lifelong Journey of Mindfulness and Meditation: In the concluding section of "Tranquil Triumphs," we'll reflect on the ongoing journey of mindfulness and meditation, emphasizing the transformative power of these practices for personal growth and well-being. You'll be encouraged to embrace the magic of mindfulness and meditation as a lifelong practice, continually deepening your connection to yourself and the world around you.

10. Additional Resources: In the appendix, you'll find a curated list of resources to support your continued exploration of mindfulness and meditation. This includes recommended books, articles, podcasts, workshops, retreats, and training programs, providing you with a wealth of information and inspiration to continue your journey.

"Tranquil Triumphs: Unleashing the Magic of Mindfulness and Meditation" is a comprehensive, practical guide that aims to empower you to harness the full potential of mindfulness and meditation in your daily life. With a blend of scientific research, personal insights, and practical techniques, this book offers a valuable resource for anyone seeking to find balance, inner peace, and happiness in today's chaotic world. By embracing the magic of mindfulness and meditation, you can experience the profound personal transformation that awaits you on this lifelong journey.

Defining mindfulness and meditation

Throughout human history, countless individuals have sought solace and wisdom in the practices of mindfulness and meditation. From the ancient traditions of the East to the bustling boardrooms of the modern world, these practices have withstood the test of time, offering a powerful pathway to inner peace, self-discovery, and personal growth. In this section, we'll explore the essence of mindfulness and meditation, providing you with a clear understanding of these transformative practices and setting the stage for your journey into their depths.

Mindfulness: The Art of Being Present

At its core, mindfulness is the practice of paying attention to the present moment in a non-judgmental, open, and curious manner. ("What are three facts about New Brunswick? – New Canadian Life") It is the art of being fully present in each moment, free from the distractions of the past and the worries of the future. Mindfulness involves cultivating an attitude of acceptance and compassion, allowing us to experience our thoughts, emotions, and physical sensations without judgment or resistance.

In today's fast-paced world, our attention is often scattered and divided, pulled in a thousand different directions at once. We become lost in the endless stream of thoughts, memories, and fantasies that dominate our minds, leaving us disconnected from the present moment and the richness of life that it holds. By practicing mindfulness, we can learn to step back from this mental whirlwind and ground ourselves in the here and now, reconnecting with the beauty, joy, and wonder that lies just beneath the surface of our everyday experiences.

Some key aspects of mindfulness practice include:

1. Paying attention: The foundation of mindfulness is the simple act of paying attention, directing our awareness to the present moment with intention and focus.
2. Non-judgment: Mindfulness involves observing our thoughts, emotions, and physical sensations without judgment or criticism, accepting them as they are without trying to change or suppress them.
3. Openness and curiosity: In practicing mindfulness, we cultivate an attitude of openness and curiosity, approaching our experiences with a sense of wonder and interest.
4. Compassion and kindness: Mindfulness encourages us to treat ourselves and others with compassion and kindness, recognizing the inherent worth and dignity of all beings.

Meditation: The Path to Inner Stillness

While mindfulness is the practice of being present in each moment, meditation is a more formal and structured approach to cultivating mindfulness and inner stillness. Meditation involves setting aside time each day to engage in specific techniques designed to focus the mind, deepen self-awareness, and promote relaxation and well-being.

There are many different forms of meditation, with roots in various spiritual and philosophical traditions. However, at their core, all meditation practices share a common goal: to train the mind and cultivate a deeper connection to our inner selves and the world around us. By engaging in meditation, we can learn to quiet the incessant chatter of our thoughts, tap into our inner wisdom, and access a wellspring of peace, joy, and resilience.

Some of the most common types of meditation include:

1. Focused attention meditation: This form of meditation involves concentrating on a single point of focus, such as the breath, a mantra, or a visual object. The goal is to train the mind to remain steady and unwavering in its attention, building mental strength and clarity.
2. Open monitoring meditation: In this style of meditation, the practitioner observes their thoughts, emotions, and sensations without judgment or attachment, allowing them to come and go without getting swept away in their content.
3. Loving-kindness meditation: Also known as "metta" meditation, this practice involves cultivating feelings of love, compassion, and goodwill toward oneself and others.

4. Body scan meditation: In this form of meditation, practitioners systematically move their attention through different parts of the body, observing any sensations, tensions, or discomfort that may arise. This practice promotes greater body awareness and can help release physical tension and stress.
5. Guided meditation: During a guided meditation, a teacher or recorded audio track provides instructions and prompts to help guide the practitioner through a specific meditation technique. This can be particularly helpful for beginners who may find it challenging to meditate without guidance.
6. Mindfulness-based stress reduction (MBSR): Developed by Jon Kabat-Zinn, MBSR is an eight-week program that combines mindfulness meditation and

yoga practices to help individuals manage stress, pain, and illness. This approach has been widely researched and has shown significant benefits for mental and physical health.

The Interplay of Mindfulness and Meditation

While mindfulness and meditation are distinct practices, they are also deeply interconnected. Mindfulness is the foundation upon which meditation is built, serving as the bedrock for the mental and emotional stability necessary to engage in more focused, structured meditation practices. At the same time, meditation can be seen as a powerful tool for deepening and refining our mindfulness skills, allowing us to access ever greater levels of presence, clarity, and insight.

As we journey through the pages of "Tranquil Triumphs: Unleashing the Magic of Mindfulness and Meditation," we'll explore the many facets of mindfulness and meditation in greater detail, delving into their history, benefits, and practical applications. We'll also introduce you to a wealth of techniques and practices designed to help you cultivate a strong, consistent mindfulness and meditation practice, tailored to your unique needs and preferences.

Whether you're a seasoned practitioner or a complete beginner, you'll find immense value in the insights and exercises presented in this book. By embracing the magic of mindfulness and meditation, you can tap into a wellspring of inner peace, joy, and resilience that will transform your life from the inside out.

As we embark on this journey together, I invite you to approach the material with an open heart and a curious mind, ready to explore the rich and varied landscape of mindfulness and meditation. In doing so, you'll discover that the true magic of these practices lies not in their esoteric origins or lofty goals, but in the simple, profound act of bringing your full attention to the present moment, and all the beauty, wisdom, and wonder it contains.

In the words of the great poet and philosopher, Rumi: "The only lasting beauty is the beauty of the heart." May your journey into the world of mindfulness and meditation bring you ever closer to the beauty of your own heart, and to the tranquillity, triumphs, and transformation that await you there.

The psychological and physiological benefits of these practices

In recent years, the ancient practices of mindfulness and meditation have garnered increasing attention from the scientific community, with a wealth of research highlighting their myriad psychological and physiological benefits. From enhancing mental health and well-being to boosting the immune system and reducing inflammation, mindfulness and meditation offer a powerful antidote to the stressors and challenges of modern life. In this section, we'll delve into the science behind these transformative practices, exploring their many benefits and the mechanisms through which they exert their effects.

Psychological Benefits of Mindfulness and Meditation

1. Reduced stress and anxiety: One of the most well-documented benefits of mindfulness and meditation is their ability to reduce stress and anxiety. By promoting relaxation and fostering a sense of calm, these practices can help to alleviate the physiological and psychological symptoms of stress, including elevated heart rate, high blood pressure, and racing thoughts. Research has shown that mindfulness and meditation can reduce cortisol

levels, the primary stress hormone, and increase resilience to stress over time.

2. Enhanced emotional regulation: Mindfulness and meditation can help individuals develop greater emotional awareness and regulation, allowing them to better understand, process, and manage their emotions. By fostering non-judgmental acceptance of our emotional experiences, these practices can help to break the cycle of rumination and emotional reactivity that often perpetuates negative emotional states.

3. Improved cognitive function: Studies have demonstrated that mindfulness and meditation can enhance various aspects of cognitive function, including attention, memory, and executive functioning. Regular meditation practice has been shown to increase the thickness of the prefrontal cortex, a region of the brain involved in complex cognitive processes such as decision-making, problem-solving, and self-regulation.

4. Greater self-awareness and self-compassion: Mindfulness and meditation can help individuals develop a deeper understanding of their thoughts, emotions, and behavioral patterns, fostering greater self-awareness and self-compassion. By cultivating an attitude of kindness and non-judgment towards ourselves, we can learn to treat ourselves with the same care and understanding that we would offer to a loved one.

5. Improved mental health and well-being: Numerous studies have demonstrated the positive effects of mindfulness and meditation on mental health and well-being. These practices have been shown to reduce symptoms of depression, anxiety, and post-traumatic stress disorder (PTSD), as well as promote overall psychological well-being and life satisfaction.

Physiological Benefits of Mindfulness and Meditation

1. Boosted immune system: Research has shown that mindfulness and meditation can have a positive impact on the immune system, increasing the production of immune cells and enhancing the body's ability to fight off infections and disease. One study found that individuals who participated in an eight-week mindfulness-based stress reduction (MBSR) program exhibited increased levels of natural killer cells, a type of immune cell that plays a critical role in combating viruses and cancer cells.

2. Reduced inflammation: Inflammation is a natural immune response that helps the body to heal and repair itself. However, chronic inflammation has been linked to a host of health problems, including heart disease, diabetes, and cancer. Studies have found that mindfulness and meditation can help to reduce inflammation by modulating the expression of genes involved in the inflammatory response.

3. Enhanced cardiovascular health: Mindfulness and meditation have been associated with a reduced risk of cardiovascular disease, the leading cause of death worldwide. These practices can help to lower blood pressure, improve heart rate variability, and decrease levels of stress hormones that can contribute to the development of heart disease.

4. Improved sleep quality: Many people struggle with sleep problems, including insomnia and poor sleep quality. Mindfulness and meditation can help to promote relaxation and improve sleep quality by reducing the racing thoughts and anxiety that often interfere with restful sleep. Studies have shown that individuals who engage in regular mindfulness and meditation practices report improved sleep quality and duration, as well as reduced daytime fatigue.

5. Pain management: Research has demonstrated that mindfulness and meditation can be effective tools for managing both acute and chronic pain. These practices can help to alter the way we perceive pain, reducing its intensity and the emotional distress associated with it. In some cases, mindfulness and meditation have been found to be as effective as traditional pain medications in reducing pain levels.

6. Enhanced neuroplasticity: The brain has an incredible ability to change and adapt throughout our lives, a process known as neuroplasticity. Mindfulness and meditation have been shown to promote neuroplasticity, increasing the brain's capacity to form new neural connections and adapt to new experiences and challenges. This can have profound implications for learning, memory, and overall cognitive function.

The Mechanisms Behind the Benefits of Mindfulness and Meditation

While the precise mechanisms through which mindfulness and meditation exert their many benefits are still being investigated, several key factors have been identified:

1. Attention regulation: One of the primary goals of mindfulness and meditation is to cultivate focused attention and awareness. By training the mind to remain present and attentive, these practices can help to strengthen our ability to regulate our attention, enhancing cognitive function and emotional regulation.

2. Body awareness: Mindfulness and meditation often involve a focus on the body, such as the breath or physical sensations. This can help to promote greater body awareness, enabling us to better understand and respond to the signals our body sends us, such as tension, pain, or hunger.

3. Emotion regulation: By fostering non-judgmental acceptance and awareness of our emotions, mindfulness and meditation can help us to develop greater emotional regulation skills. This can lead to improved mental health, well-being, and resilience in the face of life's challenges.

4. Changes in brain structure and function: Numerous studies have shown that mindfulness and meditation can lead to changes in brain structure and function, particularly in areas related to attention, emotion regulation, and self-awareness. These changes can have lasting effects on our cognitive abilities, emotional well-being, and overall mental health.

As we continue our exploration of mindfulness and meditation in "Tranquil Triumphs: Unleashing the Magic of Mindfulness and Meditation," we will delve deeper into the specific techniques and practices that can help you harness the many benefits of these ancient practices. From stress reduction and enhanced emotional regulation to improved cognitive function and overall well-being, the psychological and physiological benefits of mindfulness and meditation offer a powerful pathway to personal transformation and growth.

I encourage you to approach the material with an open mind and a willingness to experiment with the various practices and techniques presented. By doing so, you will not only gain a deeper understanding of the science behind mindfulness and meditation but also experience firsthand the profound impact these practices can have on your life. With dedication, curiosity, and an open heart, you can begin to unlock the transformative power of mindfulness and meditation, discovering a wealth of inner resources that will help you navigate the challenges and triumphs of life with grace, wisdom, and equanimity.

The impact on mental health, stress reduction, and overall well-being

The transformative power of mindfulness and meditation extends far beyond the realm of our personal experiences, having a profound and lasting impact on our mental health, stress reduction, and overall well-being. As we continue our exploration of these ancient practices in "Tranquil Triumphs: Unleashing the Magic of Mindfulness and Meditation," we'll delve into the many ways in which they can help to promote mental health and well-being, mitigate the effects of stress, and enhance our overall quality of life.

Mental Health and Mindfulness: A Powerful Partnership

In today's fast-paced, high-pressure world, the importance of mental health cannot be overstated. As rates of depression, anxiety, and other mental health disorders continue to rise, mindfulness and meditation offer a powerful and accessible means of fostering mental health and resilience.

1. Alleviating depression: Numerous studies have demonstrated the effectiveness of mindfulness and meditation in reducing symptoms of depression. By promoting greater emotional awareness and regulation, these practices can help to break the cycle of rumination and negative thinking that often perpetuates depressive symptoms. Furthermore, mindfulness-based interventions, such as mindfulness-based cognitive therapy (MBCT), have been shown to be particularly effective in preventing relapse in individuals with a history of recurrent depression.
2. Reducing anxiety: Anxiety is a pervasive issue in today's society, affecting millions of people worldwide. Mindfulness and meditation can help to reduce

anxiety by promoting relaxation, enhancing emotional regulation, and fostering a greater sense of control over one's thoughts and emotions. Studies have shown that mindfulness-based interventions, such as mindfulness-based stress reduction (MBSR), can be particularly effective in reducing symptoms of anxiety and improving overall well-being.

3. Managing post-traumatic stress disorder (PTSD): PTSD is a debilitating mental health condition that can result from exposure to traumatic events. Mindfulness and meditation have been shown to be effective tools for managing the symptoms of PTSD, including intrusive memories, avoidance behaviours, and emotional dysregulation. By promoting greater awareness and acceptance of one's thoughts and emotions, these practices can help individuals with PTSD develop healthier coping strategies and enhance their overall quality of life.

4. Boosting self-esteem: Low self-esteem can have a significant impact on our mental health and well-being, contributing to feelings of inadequacy, self-doubt, and despair. Mindfulness and meditation can help to enhance self-esteem by fostering greater self-compassion and self-acceptance, enabling us to recognize and embrace our inherent worth and value.

Stress Reduction: A Key to Well-being

In addition to their impact on mental health, mindfulness and meditation have been widely recognized for their powerful stress-reduction capabilities. By helping to mitigate the physiological and psychological effects of stress, these practices can play a critical role in promoting overall well-being and quality of life.

1. Lowering cortisol levels: Cortisol, the primary stress hormone, plays a key role in regulating our body's response to stress. Elevated cortisol levels have been linked to a host of health problems, including heart disease,

obesity, and diabetes. Research has shown that mindfulness and meditation can help to reduce cortisol levels, thereby mitigating the harmful effects of stress on our bodies and minds.

2. Improving stress resilience: In addition to reducing stress in the moment, mindfulness and meditation can help to enhance our overall resilience to stress, enabling us to better cope with the challenges and demands of everyday life. By cultivating greater self-awareness, emotional regulation, and cognitive flexibility, these practices can help us to develop healthier coping strategies and foster a more adaptive and resilient response to stressors.

3. Reducing the impact of chronic stress: Chronic stress can have a significant impact on our mental and physical health, contributing to a range of health issues, including heart disease, digestive problems, and weakened immune function. Mindfulness and meditation can help to mitigate the effects of chronic stress by promoting relaxation, enhancing emotional regulation, and fostering a greater sense of control over our thoughts and emotions. By incorporating these practices into our daily lives, we can begin to break the cycle of chronic stress and enhance our overall well-being.

Overall Well-being: The Holistic Benefits of Mindfulness and Meditation

The impact of mindfulness and meditation extends far beyond mental health and stress reduction, touching nearly every aspect of our lives. By cultivating greater awareness, presence, and compassion, these practices can help to enhance our overall well-being and quality of life.

1. Improved relationships: Mindfulness and meditation can have a significant impact on our relationships, promoting greater empathy, understanding, and

communication. By fostering greater self-awareness and emotional regulation, these practices can help us to become more attuned to the needs and experiences of others, enabling us to cultivate deeper, more meaningful connections with those around us.

2. Enhanced work performance: The benefits of mindfulness and meditation are not limited to our personal lives; they can also have a significant impact on our professional lives. Studies have shown that mindfulness and meditation can help to improve focus, attention, and productivity in the workplace, enabling us to perform more effectively and efficiently in our jobs.

3. Greater life satisfaction: By cultivating greater presence, acceptance, and gratitude, mindfulness and meditation can help to enhance our overall life satisfaction, allowing us to find greater joy, contentment, and fulfillment in our daily lives. As we learn to appreciate the beauty and richness of each moment, we can begin to tap into a wellspring of happiness and well-being that transcends the fleeting pleasures and challenges of life.

From enhancing self-esteem and fostering resilience to promoting greater life satisfaction and happiness, the benefits of mindfulness and meditation are truly transformative, offering a powerful pathway to personal growth and development for all those who practice this art.

The principles of mindfulness

As we continue our journey through "Tranquil Triumphs: Unleashing the Magic of Mindfulness and Meditation," it's essential to understand the core principles that form the foundation of mindfulness practice. These principles guide us as we cultivate greater awareness, presence, and compassion in our daily lives, providing a roadmap for personal growth and transformation.

In this chapter, we'll explore the key principles of mindfulness, examining their origins and significance as well as the practical implications they hold for our lives. By embracing these principles and integrating them into our mindfulness practice, we can begin to unlock the full potential of these ancient practices and experience the profound benefits they have to offer.

1. Non-judgment

At the heart of mindfulness lies the practice of non-judgment, which involves observing our thoughts, feelings, and experiences without labelling them as "good" or "bad," "right" or "wrong." This non-judgmental awareness allows us to cultivate a more open and accepting relationship with ourselves and our experiences, fostering greater self-compassion and understanding.

In our daily lives, we often fall into the trap of evaluating and judging our experiences, which can lead to feelings of guilt, shame, or inadequacy. By embracing the principle of non-judgment, we can learn to view our thoughts and emotions with curiosity and compassion, rather than reacting to them with judgment or aversion.

2. Patience

Patience is another essential principle of mindfulness, reflecting the understanding that personal growth and transformation are gradual, ongoing processes. By cultivating patience, we can learn to approach our mindfulness practice with an open heart and a willingness to embrace the journey, rather than focusing solely on the destination.

In our fast-paced, results-driven society, patience can often be in short supply. We may become frustrated or discouraged when we don't see immediate results or progress in our mindfulness practice. However, by embracing the principle of patience, we can learn to trust in the process and appreciate the small, incremental changes that unfold over time.

3. Beginner's Mind

The concept of the "beginner's mind" is a fundamental principle of mindfulness, encouraging us to approach each moment, experience, and situation with a fresh, open perspective. By cultivating a beginner's mind, we can learn to see the world through the eyes of a child, free from preconceptions and judgments.

In our daily lives, it's easy to become trapped in habitual patterns of thinking and perceiving, which can limit our ability to experience the full richness and beauty of the present moment. By embracing the beginner's mind, we can rediscover the wonder, curiosity, and awe that lie at the heart of mindful awareness.

4. Trust

Trust is a key principle of mindfulness, reflecting the importance of cultivating a deep sense of trust in ourselves and our inner wisdom. By trusting in our ability to navigate the complexities of our lives, we can develop greater confidence in our path and our ability to make wise, compassionate choices.

In our modern world, it's all too common to seek external validation and guidance, often at the expense of our own intuition and inner wisdom. By embracing the principle of trust, we can learn to rely on ourselves and our innate capacity for growth, healing, and transformation.

5. Non-striving

The principle of non-striving is central to mindfulness practice, reminding us that the goal of mindfulness is not to achieve some future state of enlightenment or perfection, but rather to cultivate a deep, abiding presence in the present moment. By embracing non-striving, we can learn to let go of our attachment to outcomes and expectations, freeing ourselves to fully experience and appreciate the present moment as it unfolds.

In our goal-oriented society, the idea of non-striving can seem counterintuitive or even paradoxical. However, by releasing our attachment to specific outcomes and embracing the journey itself, we can begin to experience the true power and potential of mindfulness practice. Non-striving encourages us to let go of our preconceived notions of what our practice should look like and, instead, cultivate a sense of curiosity, openness, and acceptance.

6. Acceptance

Acceptance is a fundamental principle of mindfulness, involving the practice of embracing our thoughts, feelings, and experiences just as they are, without trying to change or manipulate them. By cultivating acceptance, we can learn to develop a more compassionate and loving relationship with ourselves, our experiences, and the world around us.

In our daily lives, we often resist or avoid experiences that are uncomfortable, painful, or challenging. This resistance can create additional suffering and perpetuate unhealthy patterns of behaviour. By embracing the principle of acceptance, we can learn to meet our experiences with openness and curiosity, allowing ourselves to navigate life's challenges with greater ease and grace.

7. Letting Go

The practice of letting go is a cornerstone of mindfulness, inviting us to release our attachment to thoughts, emotions, and experiences that no longer serve us. By cultivating the ability to let go, we can learn to free ourselves from the grip of unhelpful or limiting beliefs, making space for greater clarity, wisdom, and compassion.

In our lives, we often cling to familiar patterns of thinking and behaving, even when they no longer serve our best interests. This attachment can lead to feelings of stagnation, frustration, or unhappiness. By embracing the principle of letting go, we can learn to recognize and release these unhelpful patterns, opening ourselves to new possibilities and a greater sense of freedom and well-being.

The principles of mindfulness serve as our guiding stars, helping us to navigate the complex and often challenging terrain of our inner landscape. By embracing these principles and incorporating them into our mindfulness practice, we can begin to experience the transformative power of mindfulness in our lives, unleashing the magic that lies at the heart of these ancient practices.

As you continue to explore the world of mindfulness and meditation, I encourage you to approach each moment with an open heart and a curious mind, ready to embrace the principles of mindfulness and all the wisdom, growth, and transformation they have to offer. In doing so, you'll discover that the true magic of mindfulness lies not in the attainment of some distant goal or the mastery of a particular technique, but in the simple, profound act of coming home to yourself, one breath, one moment, one heartbeat at a time.

May your journey through the world of mindfulness and meditation be filled with moments of insight, inspiration, and awakening, as you continue to uncover the boundless potential of your own heart and mind.

Integrating mindfulness into daily life

One of the most powerful aspects of mindfulness is its potential to transform our daily lives, infusing each moment with greater awareness, presence, and compassion. As we continue our journey through "Tranquil Triumphs: Unleashing the Magic of Mindfulness and Meditation," we'll explore practical strategies and techniques for integrating mindfulness into our everyday routines, helping us to cultivate a more mindful, conscious, and fulfilling life.

1. Mindful Morning Rituals

The way we begin our day can have a profound impact on our mood, energy levels, and overall well-being. By incorporating mindfulness into our morning routines, we can start each day with a clear, focused mind and a calm, open heart.

Consider the following mindful morning rituals

a. Mindful breathing: Begin your day with a few minutes of mindful breathing, focusing on the sensation of your breath as it flows in and out of your body. This simple practice can help to calm the mind and ground you in the present moment, setting the tone for a more mindful, cantered day.

b. Gratitude practice: As you wake up each morning, take a moment to reflect on the things in your life for which you are grateful. This practice can help to cultivate a more positive, appreciative mindset and foster a greater sense of well-being and happiness.

c. Mindful movement: Incorporate gentle, mindful movement into your morning routine, such as yoga, stretching, or tai chi. These practices can help to awaken the body and mind, promoting greater clarity, focus, and energy throughout the day.

2. Mindful Eating

One of the most basic and essential aspects of our daily lives is the act of eating and nourishing our bodies. By approaching mealtimes with greater mindfulness, we can foster a healthier, more conscious relationship with food and cultivate greater appreciation and enjoyment of our meals.

Consider the following mindful eating practices

a. Savouring each bite: As you eat, focus on the taste, texture, and aroma of each bite, savouring the experience fully. This practice can help to slow down the eating process, promote greater satisfaction, and reduce overeating.

b. Eating without distractions: Make a conscious effort to eat without distractions, such as television, smartphones, or other devices. By giving your full attention to the act of eating, you can cultivate a more mindful, present relationship with food.

c. Gratitude for the food: Before each meal, take a moment to express gratitude for the food you are about to eat, and the many hands and resources involved in bringing it to your plate. This practice can foster a greater sense of appreciation and connection to the food we consume.

   3. Mindful Communication

Our relationships and interactions with others are a central part of our daily lives, and mindful communication can play a critical role in fostering deeper, more meaningful connections with those around us.

Consider the following mindful communication practices:

a. Active listening: When engaging in conversation with others, make a conscious effort to listen deeply and attentively, without interrupting or formulating a response while the other person is speaking. This practice can help to promote greater understanding, empathy, and connection in our relationships.

b. Speaking with intention: Before speaking, take a moment to consider your words and their potential impact on the listener. By speaking with intention, we can cultivate greater clarity, authenticity, and compassion in our communication.

c. Mindful silence: Embrace the power of silence in your conversations, allowing for moments of stillness and reflection. This practice can help to create space for deeper listening and understanding, as well as promoting greater presence and awareness in our interactions.

4. Mindful Work and Productivity

Our work and daily tasks can provide fertile ground for mindfulness practice, offering countless opportunities to cultivate greater focus, presence, and efficiency.

Consider the following mindful work and productivity practices

a. Single-tasking: Instead of multitasking, try focusing on one task at a time, giving it your full attention and energy. This practice can help to improve productivity, reduce stress, and promote a more mindful, present approach to our daily tasks.

b. Mindful breaks: Throughout the day, take short breaks to practice mindful breathing, stretching, or simply to check in with your body and mind. These mindful breaks can help to recharge your energy, maintain focus, and prevent burnout.

c. Mindful meetings: When participating in meetings or group discussions, make a conscious effort to listen deeply, speak with intention, and remain present and engaged in the conversation. This practice can help to promote more effective, compassionate communication and collaboration in the workplace.

Mindfulness exercises and techniques for various situations

Incorporating mindfulness into our physical activities can help to enhance our overall well-being, promoting greater body awareness, presence, and enjoyment in our movement practices.

Consider the following mindful movement and exercise practices:

a. Mindful walking: When walking or hiking, focus on the sensation of your feet connecting with the ground, the rhythm of your breath, and the feeling of your body moving through space. This practice can help to ground you in the present moment and cultivate a greater sense of connection to your body and the world around you.

b. Mindful exercise: Whether you're engaging in yoga, tai chi, swimming, or other forms of exercise, approach your practice with mindfulness, focusing on the sensations and movements of your body, as well as your breath. This practice can help to enhance your enjoyment and the benefits of your physical activities.

c. Mindful stretching: Incorporate mindful stretching into your daily routine, paying close attention to the sensations in your body as you gently lengthen and release your muscles. This practice can help to improve flexibility, reduce stress, and promote greater body awareness and self-care.

Introduction to different meditation styles

As we continue our journey through the world of mindfulness and meditation, we are called to explore the diverse landscape of meditation styles, each offering its unique gifts and insights. While the foundational principles of mindfulness and presence are universal, the techniques and approaches we use to cultivate these qualities can vary widely, providing a rich tapestry of practices from which to draw inspiration and guidance.

In this chapter, we will embark on a journey through the vast array of meditation styles, exploring the unique characteristics, benefits, and challenges of each approach. As we delve into the world of meditation, we will uncover the common threads that weave through these diverse practices, as well as the unique flavours and nuances that set each style apart.

As you explore the many meditation styles presented in this chapter, I encourage you to approach your journey with an open heart and a curious mind, embracing the spirit of experimentation and discovery. As you learn about each meditation style, consider how it might resonate with your own unique interests, needs, and aspirations, and allow yourself the freedom to explore, learn, and grow as you uncover the boundless potential of your own heart and mind.

1. Mindfulness Meditation

Mindfulness meditation is perhaps the most well-known and widely practiced form of meditation in the Western world, rooted in the teachings of the Buddha and the practice of Vipassana, or insight meditation. In mindfulness meditation, we cultivate a non-judgmental, present moment awareness of our thoughts, feelings, and bodily sensations, developing greater clarity, focus, and self-awareness.

The practice of mindfulness meditation can help to cultivate greater mental and emotional resilience, reduce stress and anxiety, and promote a deeper sense of connection to ourselves and the world around us. This practice is particularly well-suited for beginners, as it provides a simple, accessible framework for developing mindfulness and presence.

2. Loving-Kindness Meditation (Metta)

Loving-kindness meditation, or Metta, is a powerful practice rooted in the Buddhist tradition, designed to cultivate feelings of love, compassion, and goodwill toward ourselves and others. In this practice, we silently repeat phrases such as "May I be happy, may I be healthy, may I be safe, may I be at ease," gradually extending these wishes to others, including loved ones, neutral individuals, and even those with whom we have difficulty.

The practice of loving-kindness meditation can help to foster greater empathy, compassion, and emotional resilience, as well as promoting a more open, loving heart. This style of meditation is especially beneficial for those who struggle with feelings of self-criticism, resentment, or anger, as it can help to soften and transform these challenging emotions.

3. Concentration Meditation (Samatha)

Concentration meditation, or Samatha, is a form of meditation that involves focusing the mind on a single point of attention, such as the breath, a mantra, or a visual object. The goal of concentration meditation is to develop a calm, focused, and stable mind, free from the distractions and fluctuations of everyday thought.

Practicing concentration meditation can help to improve mental focus, clarity, and discipline, as well as promoting a deeper sense of inner peace and tranquillity. This style of meditation can be particularly helpful for individuals who struggle with issues of attention, concentration, or restlessness, as it provides a structured framework for developing greater mental stability and control.

4. Body Scan Meditation

Body scan meditation is a form of mindfulness meditation that involves systematically directing our attention to different parts of the body, observing any sensations, tension, or discomfort that may be present. By cultivating a greater awareness of our bodily sensations, we can develop a deeper connection to our physical selves, as well as learning to recognize and release areas of tension or stress.

The practice of body scan meditation can help to promote relaxation, stress reduction, and greater body awareness, as well as fostering a more holistic, integrated sense of self. This style of meditation is particularly beneficial for those who tend to be disconnected from their bodies, or who struggle with physical tension, pain, or discomfort.

5. Guided Meditation

Guided meditation is a form of meditation in which a teacher or recording provides verbal instructions or prompts, guiding the practitioner through a specific meditation practice. This can include a wide range of techniques, such as mindfulness, visualization, or loving-kindness meditation, depending on the focus and intention of the guided meditation.

The practice of guided meditation can be especially helpful for beginners or those who struggle with maintaining focus during meditation, as it provides a structured, supportive framework for developing mindfulness and presence. Additionally, guided meditations can be a valuable tool for exploring new meditation styles or techniques, offering expert guidance and instruction along the way.

6. Transcendental Meditation

Transcendental Meditation (TM) is a form of meditation that involves the repetition of a specific mantra, or sound, which is silently repeated to help focus the mind and transcend everyday thoughts and concerns. Developed by Maharishi Mahesh Yogi in the 1950s, TM has gained widespread popularity and has been the subject of numerous scientific studies, exploring its potential benefits for mental and physical health.

Practicing Transcendental Meditation can help to promote relaxation, stress reduction, and increased mental clarity, as well as fostering a deeper sense of connection to the self and the world around us. This style of meditation may be particularly appealing to those who are drawn to mantra-based practices or who seek a more structured, formalized approach to meditation.

7. Zen Meditation (Zazen)

Zen meditation, or Zazen, is a form of meditation rooted in the Zen Buddhist tradition, which emphasizes the cultivation of a clear, present mind through the practice of seated meditation. In Zazen, practitioners often focus on the breath or the posture of the body, as well as engaging in practices such as "shikantaza," or "just sitting," which involves simply resting in the natural state of the mind, free from any specific focus or technique.

The practice of Zen meditation can help to foster greater mental clarity, focus, and presence, as well as promoting a deeper understanding of the nature of the self and reality. This style of meditation may be particularly appealing to those who are drawn to the Zen tradition or who seek a more minimalist, direct approach to meditation.

Guided meditation: benefits and examples

As we continue our exploration of the vast world of meditation, we come to the practice of guided meditation – a powerful and accessible tool for cultivating mindfulness, presence, and inner peace. In this chapter, we will delve into the many benefits of guided meditation, as well as offering examples and guidance to support you in your journey through this transformative practice.

Guided meditation provides a unique blend of structure, support, and inspiration, making it an ideal choice for beginners and experienced practitioners alike. As we journey through the landscape of guided meditation, I invite you to approach your exploration with an open heart and a curious mind, embracing the spirit of adventure and discovery as you uncover the many treasures that lie within this ancient practice.

The Benefits of Guided Meditation

The practice of guided meditation offers a wealth of benefits for both body and mind, providing a powerful framework for cultivating mindfulness, relaxation, and self-awareness. As we explore the many gifts of guided meditation, consider how these benefits might resonate with your own unique needs, interests, and aspirations.

a. Support and structure: One of the most significant benefits of guided meditation is the support and structure it provides, offering clear guidance and instruction to help you navigate the often-challenging terrain of the meditative journey. By following along with the voice of a skilled teacher or recording, you can more easily maintain focus and presence, allowing you to fully immerse yourself in the practice.

b. Accessibility: Guided meditation is an incredibly accessible practice, making it an ideal choice for beginners or those who may struggle with maintaining focus during meditation. With a wide range of guided meditations available – from short, 5-minute practices to more extended, in-depth sessions – you can easily find a meditation that suits your unique needs and schedule.

c. Variety and exploration: The world of guided meditation offers a rich tapestry of styles, techniques, and themes, allowing you to explore and experiment with a wide range of practices. From mindfulness and loving-kindness meditation to visualization and body scan techniques, guided meditation provides a wealth of opportunities for growth, discovery, and transformation.

d. Enhanced relaxation and stress reduction: Guided meditation can help to promote deeper relaxation and stress reduction, as the soothing voice of the guide helps to calm the mind and body. By following along with the guided meditation, you can more easily let go of tension, anxiety, and mental chatter, allowing you to experience a greater sense of peace and tranquillity.

e. Improved focus and mental clarity: The practice of guided meditation can help to improve focus and mental clarity, as the structured nature of the practice supports the development of greater concentration and mental discipline. By following along with the guided meditation, you can train your mind to remain more present and focused, both on and off the meditation cushion.

Examples of Guided Meditation Practices

As you embark on your journey through the world of guided meditation, consider exploring some of the following practices, each offering its unique insights and benefits:

a. Mindfulness of Breathing: This guided meditation focuses on cultivating mindfulness of the breath, helping you to develop greater focus, presence, and self-awareness. By following along with the guidance, you can learn to observe the breath with a non-judgmental, curious attitude, allowing you to experience a deeper sense of connection to the present moment.

b. Loving-Kindness Meditation: In this guided meditation, you will be guided through the practice of loving-kindness meditation, or Metta, cultivating feelings of love, compassion, and goodwill toward yourself and others. By following along with the guidance, you can learn to soften and transform feelings of self-criticism, resentment, or anger, fostering a more open, loving heart.

c. Body Scan Meditation: This guided meditation takes you on a journey through the body, systematically directing your attention to different areas and observing any sensations, tension, or discomfort that may be present. By following along with the guidance, you can develop a deeper connection to your physical self and learn to recognize and release areas of tension or stress.

d. Visualisation Meditation: In this guided meditation, you will be led through a series of visualizations designed to promote relaxation, healing, or personal growth. By following along with the guidance, you can learn to harness the power of your imagination to create positive change in your life and enhance your overall well-being.

e. Mantra Meditation: This guided meditation introduces the practice of mantra meditation, in which you silently repeat a specific word, phrase, or sound to help focus the mind and cultivate inner peace. By following along with the guidance, you can learn to use the power of sound and vibration to deepen your meditation practice and experience greater mental clarity and tranquillity.

Tips for Getting Started with Guided Meditation

As you begin your journey with guided meditation, consider the following tips to help you get started and make the most of your practice:

a. Choose a quiet, comfortable space: Find a quiet, comfortable space where you can sit or lie down without interruption. This will help you to fully immerse yourself in the guided meditation and minimize distractions.

b. Start with shorter practices: If you are new to meditation or have difficulty maintaining focus, consider starting with shorter guided meditations, such as 5-10 minute practices. As you become more comfortable and experienced with the practice, you can gradually increase the duration of your sessions.

c. Be patient and gentle with yourself: Remember that meditation is a skill that takes time and practice to develop. Be patient and gentle with yourself as you navigate the challenges and obstacles that may arise and remember that each moment of practice is an opportunity for growth and learning.

d. Experiment with different styles and techniques: The world of guided meditation offers a wealth of styles, techniques, and themes to explore. Be open to experimentation and discovery as you find the practices that resonate most deeply with your unique needs, interests, and aspirations.

e. Make a commitment to regular practice: Like any skill, meditation requires consistent practice to experience its full benefits. Make a commitment to practicing guided meditation regularly, whether daily or several times a week, to support your growth and development in this transformative practice

Developing a personal meditation practice

Developing a personal meditation practice is an essential step on the journey to inner peace, self-awareness, and spiritual growth. A personalized practice allows you to explore and deepen your relationship with meditation in a way that is uniquely attuned to your needs, interests, and aspirations. In this chapter, we will guide you through the process of creating your very own meditation sanctuary, offering tips, techniques, and inspiration to support you on your path to greater mindfulness and inner tranquillity.

Finding Your Meditation Style

The first step in developing a personal meditation practice is to discover the meditation style or technique that resonates most deeply with you. There are countless meditation styles to explore, ranging from mindfulness and loving-kindness meditation to mantra-based practices and visualization techniques. As you experiment with different styles, consider the following questions:

- What are your goals and intentions for your meditation practice? Are you seeking greater focus and mental clarity? Stress reduction and relaxation? Spiritual growth and self-awareness? Keep these goals in mind as you explore different meditation styles, seeking the practices that best align with your unique aspirations.

- How do different meditation styles make you feel? Pay attention to how you feel during and after practicing various meditation styles. Notice which practices leave you feeling calm, focused, and refreshed, and which may not resonate as deeply with you.

- Are there any specific meditation styles or traditions that you are particularly drawn to or curious about? Consider exploring these practices in greater depth, seeking out resources, teachings, or guidance to support your journey.

Creating a Consistent Practice

Consistency is key when it comes to meditation, as regular practice helps to deepen and strengthen the many benefits of mindfulness and inner peace. Consider the following tips for creating a consistent meditation practice:

- Choose a regular time to meditate each day. This might be first thing in the morning, during your lunch break, or before bedtime. By meditating at the same time each day, you can create a sense of routine and ritual around your practice.

- Start with shorter meditation sessions and gradually increase the duration over time. If you are new to meditation, begin with 5-10 minute sessions, gradually working your way up to 20-30 minutes or longer as you become more comfortable and experienced with the practice.

- Set realistic expectations for your practice. Remember that meditation is a skill that takes time and patience to develop, and that it is natural to encounter obstacles or challenges along the way. Approach your practice with a spirit of curiosity, openness, and self-compassion, recognizing that each moment of meditation is an opportunity for growth and learning.

Cultivating a Supportive Meditation Environment

Creating a supportive environment for your meditation practice can help to enhance your experience and deepen your connection to mindfulness and inner peace. Consider the following tips for cultivating a meditation sanctuary:

- Choose a quiet, comfortable space in your home where you can sit or lie down without interruption. This might be a dedicated meditation room, a quiet corner of your bedroom, or any other space that feels calm and inviting.
- Personalize your meditation space with meaningful items or decorations, such as candles, incense, crystals, or spiritual artwork. These items can help to create a sense of sacredness and intention around your practice.
- Consider using a meditation cushion, chair, or mat to support your body during your practice. This can help to promote proper posture and alignment, making it easier to maintain focus and presence during meditation.
4. Deepening Your Practice: Resources and Support

As you continue to develop and refine your personal meditation practice, consider seeking out additional resources and support to help deepen your understanding and experience of meditation. There are countless books, articles, online courses, and guided meditation recordings available to support you on your journey. Here are some suggestions for deepening your practice:

a. Books and articles: Explore a variety of books and articles on meditation, mindfulness, and related topics. Look for works by renowned meditation teachers, such as Thich Nhat Hanh, Pema Chödrön, Jack Kornfield, Jon Kabat-Zinn, and Sharon Salzberg, among others. These authors offer valuable insights and guidance for deepening your understanding and experience of meditation.

b. Online courses and workshops: Many meditation teachers and organizations offer online courses, workshops, and retreats that can provide more structured and in-depth guidance for your practice. Consider signing up for a course that aligns with your interests and goals, such as a mindfulness-based stress reduction (MBSR) course or a loving-kindness meditation workshop.

c. Guided meditation recordings: Guided meditation recordings can be a valuable resource for deepening your practice, offering step-by-step instructions and support for a variety of meditation techniques. Explore different guided meditation recordings to find the ones that resonate most deeply with your unique needs and aspirations.

d. Local meditation groups and communities: Connecting with a local meditation group or community can provide valuable support, encouragement, and inspiration for your practice. Seek out meditation centres, yoga studios, or spiritual communities in your area that offer group meditation sessions or workshops. Practicing with others can help to strengthen your commitment to your practice and provide a sense of connection and shared purpose.

e. Meditation retreats: Attending a meditation retreat can be a transformative experience, offering an immersive environment for deepening your practice and understanding of meditation. Many meditation centres and spiritual communities offer retreats ranging from weekend workshops to week-long or even month-long intensive programs. Consider attending a retreat that aligns with your interests, goals, and schedule to further enrich your meditation journey.

Overcoming Common Challenges

Addressing misconceptions about meditation and mindfulness
Demystifying Meditation: Dispelling Myths and Embracing the Truth

As the popularity of meditation and mindfulness continues to grow, so too do the misconceptions and misunderstandings surround these transformative practices. For those new to meditation, these myths and misconceptions can be confusing or even discouraging, preventing them from fully experiencing the myriad benefits of mindfulness and inner peace. In this chapter, we will address some common misconceptions about meditation and mindfulness, revealing the truth behind these powerful practices and inviting you to embrace the journey with an open heart and a curious mind.

1. Myth: Meditation is about emptying your mind of thoughts.

One of the most pervasive misconceptions about meditation is that it involves emptying your mind of all thoughts, achieving a state of complete mental silence. This misunderstanding can lead to frustration and self-judgment when thoughts inevitably arise during meditation.

Truth: Meditation is about cultivating awareness of your thoughts and learning to observe them without judgment. Rather than trying to eliminate thoughts, the aim of meditation is to develop mindfulness – the ability to observe your thoughts, emotions, and bodily sensations with curiosity and non-judgmental awareness. By practicing this skill, you can learn to disengage from the constant stream of mental chatter and experience a greater sense of inner peace and tranquillity.

2. Myth: You need to sit in a specific posture to meditate.

Many people believe that meditation requires sitting in a particular posture, such as the classic cross-legged position or the lotus pose. This misconception can be discouraging for those who find these positions uncomfortable or difficult to maintain for extended periods.

Truth: There is no one "correct" posture for meditation. The key is to find a position that allows you to remain comfortable, relaxed, and alert. This might involve sitting in a chair, lying down, or even walking or standing. The most important aspect of your meditation posture is maintaining an upright, alert posture, which supports focus and concentration while also promoting relaxation and ease.

3. Myth: You need to meditate for long periods to experience benefits.

Some people assume that meditation requires lengthy, time-consuming sessions in order to be effective. This belief can be particularly discouraging for those with busy schedules or limited time for self-care.

Truth: Even short, consistent meditation sessions can yield significant benefits. While longer meditation sessions can be valuable for deepening your practice and understanding, even just a few minutes of daily meditation can help to reduce stress, improve focus, and enhance overall well-being. The key is to develop a consistent practice, whether that involves 5 minutes or 50 minutes of meditation each day.

4. Myth: Meditation is a religious or spiritual practice.

While meditation has its roots in various spiritual and religious traditions, it is often mistakenly assumed that meditation is exclusively a religious or spiritual practice. This misconception can be off-putting for those who do not identify with a particular religious or spiritual tradition or who are simply seeking a secular means of stress reduction and self-improvement.

Truth: Meditation can be practiced by anyone, regardless of their religious or spiritual beliefs. While meditation is indeed an integral part of many spiritual traditions, it is also a valuable tool for cultivating mindfulness, relaxation, and self-awareness that transcends religious boundaries. Many secular approaches to meditation, such as mindfulness-based stress reduction (MBSR), have been developed to make the practice accessible and relevant to a diverse range of individuals and communities.

5. Myth: Only certain types of people can benefit from meditation.

Some people may believe that meditation is only suitable for certain types of individuals, such as those who are naturally calm, introverted, or spiritually inclined. This misconception can prevent people from exploring meditation, assuming
that it is not a suitable practice for them or that they will not benefit from it.

Truth: Meditation is a universal practice that can benefit anyone, regardless of personality, background, or lifestyle. People from all walks of life and with diverse personal characteristics can experience the transformative effects of meditation, including reduced stress, improved mental clarity, and enhanced emotional well-being. The beauty of meditation lies in its adaptability and inclusiveness, offering a wide range of techniques and approaches to suit individual needs, preferences, and goals.

6. Myth: If you don't experience immediate results, meditation isn't working.

Some people may become discouraged if they don't experience immediate or dramatic results from their meditation practice. They may assume that they are not "good" at meditation or that the practice simply doesn't work for them.

Truth: Meditation is a skill that takes time, patience, and consistent practice to develop. Like any other skill, the benefits of meditation often unfold gradually over time as you deepen your understanding and experience of the practice. It is important to approach meditation with realistic expectations and a willingness to be patient with yourself and the process. Remember that the journey is just as important as the destination, and that each moment of meditation offers an opportunity for growth, learning, and self-discovery.

7. Myth: Meditation is a form of escapism or avoidance.

Some people may view meditation as a form of escapism or avoidance, a way of disengaging from the challenges and responsibilities of daily life. This misconception can lead to scepticism about the value and purpose of meditation, particularly in the context of personal growth and self-improvement.

Truth: Meditation is not about escaping or avoiding reality, but rather about cultivating a deeper, more mindful engagement with life. Through the practice of meditation, you can develop greater self-awareness, emotional resilience, and mental clarity, which can help you navigate the complexities and challenges of life with greater skill and grace. By fostering a deeper connection to your inner world, meditation can actually enhance your ability to engage with the world around you in a more meaningful, authentic, and compassionate way.

By addressing and dispelling these common misconceptions about meditation and mindfulness, we can create a more accurate and empowering understanding of these transformative practices.

Dealing with a wandering mind and distractions

Understanding the Nature of the Wandering Mind

The concept of the "monkey mind"

The "monkey mind" is a term often used in meditation and mindfulness circles to describe the restless, agitated, and constantly shifting nature of our thoughts. It is derived from the ancient Buddhist concept of "kapicitta," which refers to the unsettled and wandering state of the human mind. Just like a monkey swinging from branch to branch, our thoughts tend to jump from one idea to another, making it difficult for us to concentrate and find inner peace.

The monkey mind is often seen as an obstacle in meditation and mindfulness practices, as it can create feelings of frustration and impatience when we're unable to focus our attention. However, understanding the monkey mind is an essential part of our personal growth and development. Recognizing that the monkey mind is a natural aspect of human cognition can help us approach our practice with greater patience, self-compassion, and acceptance.

One of the main goals of mindfulness and meditation is to tame the monkey mind by gently guiding our attention back to the present moment, allowing us to cultivate greater awareness, concentration, and inner tranquillity. This is not about suppressing or eliminating our thoughts, but rather about developing a more balanced and harmonious relationship with our minds. By observing our thoughts without judgment or attachment, we can create space for clarity, insight, and a deeper understanding of ourselves and the world around us.

Some techniques to help tame the monkey mind include:

1. Focused Attention Meditation: Concentrating on a single point of focus, such as the breath, a mantra, or a physical object, can help train the mind to stay present and attentive.
2. Open Monitoring Meditation: This practice involves observing thoughts, feelings, and bodily sensations without judgment or attachment, allowing the mind to settle naturally over time.
3. Body Scan Meditation: By directing our attention to different parts of the body and observing any sensations or tension present, we can anchor our awareness in the physical realm and cultivate a greater sense of calm.
4. Loving-Kindness Meditation: This practice involves directing feelings of love, compassion, and goodwill toward ourselves and others, which can help soothe the agitated monkey mind and cultivate a more balanced and compassionate perspective.

As we become more familiar with our thought patterns and learn to gently guide our attention back to the present moment, we can experience greater peace, focus, and well-being in our daily lives.

The impact of modern distractions on our attention span

In today's fast-paced and technology-driven world, we are constantly bombarded with information, stimuli, and distractions. This constant influx of distractions has a profound impact on our attention span, making it even more challenging to maintain focus and cultivate mindfulness.

1. Information Overload: The internet, social media, and 24-hour news cycles expose us to an unprecedented amount of information, making it difficult for our minds to process and retain everything. This constant barrage of data can lead to mental fatigue, stress, and a reduced ability to concentrate on a single task or thought.

2. Multitasking: The prevalence of digital devices and the expectation to be constantly connected have led many people to multitask in an attempt to keep up with the demands of modern life. Research shows that multitasking is inefficient and negatively affects our cognitive abilities, causing us to lose focus more easily and struggle with concentrating on a single task.

3. Instant Gratification: Our modern culture often prioritizes speed and convenience, fostering a desire for instant gratification. This can result in a shorter attention span and an inability to engage in activities that require patience and sustained focus, such as meditation and deep reflection.

4. Fragmented Attention: The constant interruptions from notifications, messages, and alerts on our digital devices can lead to fragmented

attention, making it more challenging to fully engage with the present moment or immerse ourselves in a single activity. This state of continuous partial attention can contribute to feelings of restlessness and dissatisfaction.

Despite these challenges, it is possible to mitigate the impact of modern distractions on our attention span by cultivating mindfulness and incorporating meditation practices into our daily lives. Here are some strategies to help reduce distractions and improve focus:

1. Establish Boundaries: Set limits on your screen time and create designated periods for checking email, social media, and other digital distractions. Consider turning off non-essential notifications and using "Do Not Disturb" mode during meditation or other focused activities.
2. Create a Mindful Environment: Designate a quiet, clutter-free space for meditation and other mindful activities to minimize distractions and encourage focus. You can also incorporate elements such as calming scents or soothing sounds to enhance the ambiance.
3. Practice Single-Tasking: Resist the urge to multitask and dedicate your full attention to one activity at a time. This will help train your mind to focus more effectively and can improve productivity and mental clarity.
4. Develop a Consistent Meditation Practice: Engaging in regular meditation can help strengthen your ability to concentrate and increase your overall attention span. Experiment with different meditation techniques to find the one that best suits your needs and preferences.
5. Incorporate Mindfulness into Daily Activities: Practice being fully present and engaged during everyday tasks, such as eating, walking, or washing

dishes. This can help you become more accustomed to focusing on the present moment, even amidst the distractions of modern life.

By actively addressing the impact of modern distractions on our attention span and cultivating mindfulness, we can develop a greater sense of focus, clarity, and inner peace.

Accepting the wandering mind as a natural phenomenon

One of the keys to successful mindfulness and meditation practice is recognizing and accepting the wandering mind as a natural part of human cognition. Our minds are constantly processing information, generating thoughts, and making connections, which can lead to a seemingly endless stream of mental chatter. Instead of viewing the wandering mind as a failure or obstacle, we can approach it with curiosity, patience, and understanding.

Here are some strategies for accepting the wandering mind as a natural phenomenon:

1. Cultivate Non-Judgment: Approach your thoughts and mental wanderings with a sense of curiosity and openness, without labelling them as good or bad. This non-judgmental awareness allows you to observe your thoughts without getting caught up in them, fostering a more balanced and mindful state of mind.
2. Develop Self-Compassion: Be kind and patient with yourself as you practice mindfulness and meditation. Recognize that a wandering mind is a common

experience for everyone and that it takes time and consistent practice to develop greater focus and concentration.

3. Embrace Impermanence: Understand that thoughts, emotions, and sensations are temporary and ever-changing. By recognizing the transient nature of our mental experiences, we can learn to let go of our attachment to them and develop a more grounded and present awareness.

4. Use the Breath as an Anchor: When you notice your mind wandering, gently guide your attention back to the breath or another point of focus. This process of returning to the present moment helps to train the mind to be more attentive and aware.

5. Reframe Distractions: Instead of viewing distractions as obstacles, consider them as opportunities to practice mindfulness and strengthen your mental focus. Each time you notice your mind wandering and bring your attention back to the present, you are honing your skills in concentration and self-awareness.

6. Recognize the Benefits: Understand that even when your mind wanders, you are still reaping the benefits of meditation and mindfulness practice. Research shows that regular meditation can improve cognitive function, emotional well-being, and physical health, even if the mind wanders during practice.

By accepting the wandering mind as a natural phenomenon, we can approach our mindfulness and meditation practice with greater patience, understanding, and self-compassion. This attitude allows us to cultivate a deeper connection with our inner selves and experience the transformative benefits of these practices, ultimately leading to greater inner peace and well-being.

Establishing consistency in your practice

Establishing consistency in your mindfulness and meditation practice is crucial for reaping the maximum benefits and making it an integral part of your daily routine. Consistency helps train the mind, develop discipline, and create lasting positive changes in your mental, emotional, and physical well-being. Here are some tips for establishing consistency in your practice:

1. Set a Regular Schedule: Choose a specific time each day to meditate and stick to that schedule as much as possible. Many people find it helpful to meditate first thing in the morning or just before bedtime, as these are generally quieter periods with fewer distractions.
2. Start Small: Begin with short meditation sessions and gradually increase the duration as you become more comfortable and accustomed to the practice. Even just 5-10 minutes per day can have a significant impact on your well-being.
3. Create a Dedicated Space: Designate a quiet, comfortable space in your home for meditation and mindfulness practice. This can help signal to your brain that it's time to focus and be present, making it easier to transition into a meditative state.
4. Establish a Routine: Incorporate meditation into your daily routine, just like brushing your teeth or having breakfast. This can help make it a non-negotiable habit, ensuring that you prioritize your practice even on busy days.

5. Use Reminders: Set reminders on your phone, leave notes around your living space, or use a meditation app to help you stay accountable and remember to practice daily.

6. Be Flexible: While it's important to establish a consistent schedule, it's also essential to be flexible and adaptable. If you miss a session or your routine is disrupted, don't be too hard on yourself. Simply acknowledge the situation and return to your practice as soon as possible.

7. Connect with a Community: Join a meditation group or connect with like-minded individuals online to share experiences, ask questions, and stay motivated. The support and encouragement of a community can help you stay committed to your practice.

8. Set Realistic Expectations: Remember that meditation is a lifelong journey, and progress may be gradual. Be patient with yourself, and don't expect immediate results. Consistency and perseverance are key to experiencing the long-term benefits of mindfulness and meditation.

9. Track Your Progress: Keep a journal or use an app to track your meditation practice, noting the duration, frequency, and any insights or challenges you encounter. This can help you stay motivated and provide a sense of accomplishment as you witness your progress over time.

10. Make It Enjoyable: Experiment with different meditation techniques and find one that resonates with you and feels enjoyable. You're more likely to be consistent with your practice if you look forward to it and find it personally fulfilling.

By establishing consistency in your mindfulness and meditation practice, you'll be better equipped to experience the transformative effects of these practices, leading to enhanced well-being, inner peace, and personal growth.

Mindfulness and Meditation for Stress Management

Understanding Stress and Its Effects on the Mind and Body

Stress is a natural and inevitable part of life, arising from various sources such as work, relationships, finances, and personal challenges. While a certain degree of stress can be beneficial in motivating us to take action and adapt to new situations, chronic stress can have significant negative effects on both our mental and physical well-being.

1. Psychological Effects of Stress: a. Anxiety and worry: Chronic stress can lead to persistent feelings of anxiety, making it difficult to relax or focus on the present moment. b. Irritability and mood swings: Stress can cause heightened emotional sensitivity, leading to irritability, anger, or mood swings. c. Depression: Prolonged stress can contribute to feelings of hopelessness, sadness, and a lack of motivation or enjoyment in daily activities. d. Impaired cognitive function: Stress can negatively affect memory, concentration, and decision-making abilities. e. Sleep disturbances: High stress levels can lead to insomnia or disrupted sleep patterns, further exacerbating mental and emotional strain.

2. Physical Effects of Stress: a. Immune system suppression: Chronic stress can weaken the immune system, making the body more susceptible to infections and illnesses. b. Cardiovascular issues: Stress can contribute to increased blood pressure, elevated heart rate, and a higher risk of heart disease. c. Digestive problems: Stress can lead to gastrointestinal issues such as indigestion, stomach pain, or changes in appetite. d. Musculoskeletal tension: Stress often manifests as physical tension in the

body, leading to muscle aches, stiffness, and pain. e. Hormonal imbalances: Prolonged stress can disrupt the body's hormonal balance, leading to various health issues and exacerbating pre-existing conditions.

Understanding the effects of stress on the mind and body is crucial for implementing effective coping strategies and promoting overall well-being. Mindfulness and meditation practices can be powerful tools for managing stress and mitigating its negative impacts. By cultivating awareness, self-compassion, and mental resilience, we can better navigate life's challenges and maintain a sense of balance and inner peace.

Techniques for using mindfulness and meditation to reduce stress

Using mindfulness and meditation techniques to reduce stress can help you develop greater resilience, emotional balance, and overall well-being. Here are some effective techniques to incorporate into your daily routine:

1. Mindful Breathing: Focus on your breath as it flows in and out of your body. This simple practice can help you anchor your attention in the present moment, quiet the mind, and reduce stress.
2. Body Scan Meditation: Lie down or sit comfortably and mentally scan your body from head to toe, observing any sensations, tension, or discomfort. This practice can help you develop greater awareness of your physical state and release stress-related tension.
3. Loving-Kindness Meditation (Metta): Cultivate feelings of love and compassion for yourself and others by silently repeating phrases such as "May I be happy, may I be healthy, may I be safe, may I be at ease." This

practice can help you develop a more compassionate and supportive inner dialogue, reducing stress and fostering emotional well-being.

4. Progressive Muscle Relaxation: Tense and relax different muscle groups throughout your body in a systematic manner, starting from your toes and working up to your head. This technique can help you release physical tension and stress, promoting relaxation and mental calm.

5. Visualization: Close your eyes and imagine yourself in a peaceful, soothing environment, such as a beach or a forest. Engage all of your senses and immerse yourself in the calming atmosphere, allowing stress to dissipate as you focus on the serene setting.

6. Mindful Movement: Incorporate mindfulness into physical activities such as yoga, tai chi, or walking. By focusing on your breath and body sensations during movement, you can develop greater awareness and reduce stress.

7. Guided Meditation: Listen to a recorded meditation or use a meditation app that guides you through stress-reduction techniques. This can be particularly helpful for beginners or those who struggle to meditate independently.

8. Three-Minute Breathing Space: Whenever you notice feelings of stress or overwhelm, take a brief pause to check in with your breath, body sensations, and thoughts. This can help you acknowledge and diffuse stress before it escalates.

9. Journaling: Write down your thoughts, emotions, and experiences as a form of mindfulness practice. This can help you process and release stress, gain insight, and develop greater self-awareness.

10. Establish a Regular Meditation Routine: Make a commitment to practice meditation or mindfulness techniques daily, even if it's just for a few

minutes. Consistency is key to reaping the stress-reducing benefits of these practices.

By incorporating these mindfulness and meditation techniques into your daily life, you can reduce stress, enhance emotional resilience, and cultivate a greater sense of inner peace and well-being.

Developing a personalized stress management plan

Creating a personalized stress management plan is essential for effectively dealing with stress and promoting overall well-being. By identifying the unique sources of stress in your life and implementing tailored strategies to address them, you can cultivate greater resilience and balance. Here are some steps to develop your own stress management plan:

1. Assess Your Stressors: Make a list of the stressors in your life, both big and small. Be honest and thorough in your evaluation, considering all aspects of your life, including work, relationships, finances, health, and personal goals.
2. Prioritize: Rank your stressors based on their impact on your well-being and the level of control you have over them. This can help you determine which issues to address first and which ones may require more long-term solutions.
3. Identify Your Coping Strategies: Reflect on how you currently cope with stress and determine which strategies are helpful and which may be counterproductive. By recognizing your existing coping mechanisms, you can build on the effective ones and replace or modify the unhelpful ones.
4. Set Realistic Goals: Establish achievable goals for managing your stress, focusing on small, incremental changes that can lead to significant

improvements over time. Avoid setting overly ambitious goals, as this can lead to additional stress and frustration.

5. Incorporate Mindfulness and Meditation Techniques: Choose one or more of the mindfulness and meditation techniques discussed earlier and integrate them into your daily routine. Regular practice is key to reaping the stress-reducing benefits of these practices.

6. Develop Healthy Habits: Incorporate healthy lifestyle habits into your stress management plan, such as regular exercise, a balanced diet, and adequate sleep. These habits can help support your physical and mental well-being, making it easier to manage stress.

7. Seek Support: Connect with friends, family members, or professionals who can provide emotional support, encouragement, and guidance. Sharing your experiences and receiving feedback can help you stay motivated and accountable in your stress management efforts.

8. Monitor Your Progress: Periodically review your stress management plan and assess your progress. Make adjustments as needed, incorporating new strategies and techniques that may be beneficial for your unique circumstances.

9. Practice Self-Compassion: Be kind and patient with yourself as you work on managing your stress. Remember that change takes time and that setbacks are a natural part of the process. Cultivating self-compassion can help you maintain a positive outlook and stay committed to your stress management plan.

10. Stay Flexible: Be willing to adapt and modify your plan as needed, recognizing that life circumstances and stressors may change over time. Maintaining a flexible approach to stress management can help you navigate challenges more effectively and foster greater resilience.

By developing a personalized stress management plan, you can take control of your well-being and cultivate greater resilience, balance, and inner peace. Remember that managing stress is an ongoing process, and your plan should evolve and adapt as your life circumstances change.

Enhancing Emotional Intelligence and Self-Awareness

The Role of Mindfulness and Meditation in Emotional Intelligence

Emotional intelligence (EI) refers to the ability to recognize, understand, and manage one's own emotions and those of others. ("Taking Emotional Intelligence to Work - LinkedIn") Mindfulness and meditation play a significant role in developing and enhancing emotional intelligence through the following ways:

1. Self-awareness: Mindfulness practices, such as focused attention on the breath or body sensations, can increase self-awareness by helping individuals become more in tune with their internal experiences, including emotions. This heightened awareness allows individuals to better understand their emotional triggers and patterns, which is a crucial component of emotional intelligence.

2. Emotional Regulation: Mindfulness meditation encourages individuals to observe their emotions without judgment or reactivity. By cultivating a non-judgmental attitude towards one's emotions, individuals can learn to respond to emotional experiences more skilfully and effectively, rather than being controlled by them.

3. Empathy and Compassion: Loving-kindness (Metta) meditation and other compassion-based practices can help individuals develop a greater sense of empathy and understanding for the emotions and experiences of others. This increased empathy and compassion can lead to improved interpersonal relationships and a stronger ability to navigate social situations.

4. Reduced Stress and Anxiety: Mindfulness and meditation practices have been shown to reduce stress and anxiety, both of which can interfere with emotional intelligence. By reducing stress and anxiety, individuals are better able to maintain emotional balance and respond to situations in a more thoughtful and considered manner.

5. Improved Focus and Concentration: Mindfulness and meditation practices can enhance focus and concentration, allowing individuals to be more present and attentive in their interactions with others. This increased presence can lead to better communication and understanding, fostering stronger emotional connections.

6. Enhanced Resilience: Mindfulness and meditation practices can help individuals develop greater emotional resilience, allowing them to bounce back more quickly from negative emotional experiences or setbacks. This increased resilience can lead to a greater ability to adapt and cope with emotional challenges, which is an essential component of emotional intelligence.

Techniques for Improving Self-Awareness and Self-Regulation

Improving self-awareness and self-regulation is key to fostering emotional intelligence and personal growth. Here are some techniques that can help enhance these essential skills:

1. Mindful Breathing: Focus on your breath as it naturally flows in and out of your body. This simple mindfulness practice can help you cultivate greater self-awareness and anchor your attention to the present moment. By returning to your breath when you notice your mind wandering, you can develop the ability to regulate your attention and emotions more effectively.

2. Body Scan Meditation: This meditation technique involves systematically bringing your attention to different parts of your body, observing sensations without judgment. This practice can help you become more aware of your physical and emotional states, allowing you to recognize and regulate your emotions more effectively.

3. Journaling: Writing about your thoughts, emotions, and experiences can be a powerful tool for enhancing self-awareness. By reflecting on your emotions and identifying patterns, you can gain insights into your emotional triggers and develop strategies for self-regulation.

4. Emotional Check-ins: Set aside time throughout the day to pause and reflect on your current emotional state. This practice can help you become more aware of your emotions, allowing you to address and regulate them more effectively.

5. Mindful Listening: Practice actively listening to others, focusing on their words, tone, and body language without judgment. This technique can help improve your self-awareness by fostering empathy and understanding, which in turn can contribute to better self-regulation.

6. Cognitive Reappraisal: Learn to reframe negative thoughts or situations in a more balanced or positive light. This cognitive skill can help you regulate your emotions by challenging unhelpful thought patterns and fostering a more adaptive perspective.

7. Practicing Self-Compassion: Develop a kind, non-judgmental attitude towards yourself and your emotions. By cultivating self-compassion, you can better understand and accept your emotional experiences, leading to more effective self-regulation.

8. Setting Boundaries: Establish and maintain healthy boundaries in your relationships and daily life. By setting boundaries, you can create a supportive environment for self-awareness and self-regulation.

9. Engaging in Mindful Activities: Participate in activities that require focus and presence, such as yoga, tai chi, or art. These practices can help you cultivate greater self-awareness and self-regulation by requiring you to be fully present and engaged.

10. Seeking Professional Support: Consider working with a therapist or coach to help you develop self-awareness and self-regulation skills. A professional can offer guidance, support, and tools tailored to your individual needs and goals.

By incorporating these techniques into your daily life, you can improve your self-awareness and self-regulation, ultimately enhancing your emotional intelligence and overall well-being.

Cultivating Empathy and Compassion through Mindfulness

Empathy and compassion are essential components of emotional intelligence and play a crucial role in building healthy relationships and fostering overall well-being. Mindfulness practices can help you cultivate empathy and compassion in the following ways:

1. Loving-Kindness (Metta) Meditation: This meditation practice involves silently repeating phrases, such as "May I/you be happy, may I/you be healthy, may I/you be safe, may I/you live with ease," while focusing on yourself or others. This practice helps to cultivate feelings of warmth, kindness, and compassion towards oneself and others.

2. Tonglen Meditation: This practice involves visualizing taking in the suffering of others on the in-breath and sending out relief, love, and compassion on the out-breath. This can help you develop empathy and compassion by actively engaging with the suffering of others.

3. Mindful Listening: Practice active listening by giving your full attention to others when they are speaking, without interrupting or judging. By being fully present and attentive, you can better understand the emotions and experiences of others, fostering empathy and compassion.

4. Developing Non-Judgmental Awareness: Cultivate a non-judgmental attitude towards your thoughts, emotions, and experiences, as well as those of others. By practicing non-judgment, you can develop a greater understanding and acceptance of the emotions and perspectives of others, which can lead to increased empathy and compassion.

5. Cultivating Gratitude: Practice gratitude by reflecting on the positive aspects of your life and the kindness of others. This can help you foster a sense of

connection and compassion towards others by recognizing the interdependence of all beings.

6. Practicing Perspective-Taking: Make an effort to see situations from another person's point of view. By trying to understand the emotions, thoughts, and experiences of others, you can develop greater empathy and compassion.

7. Engaging in Compassionate Action: Look for opportunities to help others in need, whether it's through volunteering, offering emotional support, or simply lending a hand. Acts of kindness and service can help you cultivate empathy and compassion by directly connecting you with the experiences of others.

8. Mindful Self-Compassion: Develop a kind and understanding attitude towards your own emotions and experiences. By cultivating self-compassion, you can better empathize with the suffering of others and respond with genuine care and concern.

By incorporating these mindfulness practices into your daily life, you can develop greater empathy and compassion for yourself and others. This can lead to improved emotional intelligence, stronger relationships, and enhanced overall well-being.

Mindfulness and Meditation in Relationships

The Benefits of Mindfulness and Meditation for Interpersonal Connections

Mindfulness and meditation practices can have a profound impact on interpersonal connections by fostering greater emotional intelligence, empathy, and communication skills. Here are some of the key benefits of mindfulness and meditation for improving interpersonal relationships:

1. Enhanced Emotional Intelligence: As discussed earlier, mindfulness and meditation practices can help you develop greater self-awareness, self-regulation, empathy, and compassion. These skills are essential components of emotional intelligence, which is crucial for navigating and maintaining healthy interpersonal connections.

2. Improved Communication Skills: Mindfulness practices, such as mindful listening and non-judgmental awareness, can significantly improve your communication skills. By being fully present and attentive in your interactions, you can develop a deeper understanding of others' emotions and perspectives, leading to more effective and empathetic communication.

3. Reduced Reactivity and Conflict Resolution: Mindfulness and meditation can help you develop greater emotional regulation, which can reduce reactivity in your relationships. By responding to situations with a calm and balanced mindset, you can better navigate conflicts and resolve issues in a more constructive manner.

4. Increased Empathy and Compassion: As previously mentioned, mindfulness and meditation practices can help you cultivate greater empathy and compassion for yourself and others. This increased understanding and concern for others' emotions and experiences can lead to stronger interpersonal connections and more supportive relationships.

5. Greater Presence and Attunement: Mindfulness and meditation practices can help you become more present and attuned to the needs and emotions of others. By being fully engaged and attentive in your interactions, you can develop deeper connections and foster a greater sense of trust and intimacy in your relationships.

6. Enhanced Emotional Resilience: Mindfulness and meditation can help you build emotional resilience, allowing you to better cope with stress, setbacks,

and emotional challenges in your relationships. This increased resilience can lead to healthier and more adaptive interpersonal connections.

7. Strengthened Bonds and Social Support: By fostering greater emotional intelligence, empathy, and communication skills, mindfulness and meditation can help you develop stronger bonds and social support networks. These connections are essential for overall well-being and can provide a foundation for navigating life's challenges.

By incorporating mindfulness and meditation practices into your daily routine, you can experience numerous benefits for your interpersonal connections, including improved emotional intelligence, communication skills, empathy, and emotional resilience. These skills can enhance the quality of your relationships and contribute to greater life satisfaction and overall well-being.

Techniques for Mindful Communication and Active Listening

Mindful communication and active listening are essential for fostering strong interpersonal connections and enhancing emotional intelligence. Here are some techniques to help you practice mindful communication and active listening:

1. Be fully present: When engaging in conversation, give your full attention to the person you're speaking with. Focus on their words, tone of voice, and body language, while minimizing distractions and setting aside your own thoughts and concerns.

2. Practice non-judgmental awareness: Approach conversations with an open mind and a non-judgmental attitude. This means suspending your assumptions and biases, and genuinely trying to understand the other person's perspective without immediately evaluating or categorizing it.

3. Use reflective listening: Reflect back what you've heard to ensure you've accurately understood the speaker's message. You can do this by paraphrasing their words or summarizing their main points. This technique demonstrates that you are actively listening and helps to clarify any potential misunderstandings.

4. Validate emotions and feelings: Acknowledge and validate the other person's emotions by expressing empathy and understanding. You can do this by saying things like, "I can see how you would feel that way" or "That must have been difficult for you." Validating emotions helps to create a safe space for open communication.

5. Use "I" statements: When expressing your thoughts and feelings, use "I" statements instead of "you" statements. ("Using "I" Statements to Communicate Effectively") This helps to avoid placing blame or making accusations and promotes a more constructive conversation. For example, say, "I feel frustrated when…" instead of "You make me feel frustrated when…"

6. Ask open-ended questions: Encourage the speaker to share more information by asking open-ended questions that cannot be answered with a simple "yes" or "no." These questions invite deeper exploration and promote a more meaningful conversation.

7. Offer appropriate feedback: Provide constructive feedback that is specific, timely, and relevant. Be mindful of the tone and language you use when offering feedback to ensure it is helpful and supportive.

8. Cultivate patience and silence: Practice patience in your conversations, giving the other person time to gather their thoughts and express themselves. Embrace moments of silence, which can provide a valuable opportunity for reflection and deeper understanding.

9. Be aware of nonverbal cues: Pay attention to body language, facial expressions, and other nonverbal cues, which can provide valuable insights into the other person's feelings and emotions. Adjust your own nonverbal communication to convey empathy, openness, and understanding.
10. Practice self-awareness: Develop an awareness of your own communication patterns and habits, including any tendencies to interrupt, judge, or dominate the conversation. By becoming more self-aware, you can work on improving your communication skills and fostering more authentic and meaningful connections.

By incorporating these techniques into your daily interactions, you can enhance your mindful communication and active listening skills, leading to stronger interpersonal connections, improved emotional intelligence, and greater overall well-being.

Fostering Stronger Relationships through Shared Mindfulness Practices

Sharing mindfulness practices with your friends, family, or romantic partners can significantly enhance your interpersonal connections by promoting mutual understanding, empathy, and support. Here are some ways to foster stronger relationships through shared mindfulness practices:

1. Partner Meditation: Engage in meditation sessions together, either by sitting side by side or facing each other. This shared practice can create a sense of connection, calmness, and presence, strengthening the bond between you and your partner.
2. Mindful Walking: Go for a mindful walk together, paying attention to your surroundings, your body movements, and your breath. This shared

experience can help you cultivate presence and appreciation for the present moment, fostering a deeper connection with one another.

3. Loving-Kindness Meditation: Practice loving-kindness (Metta) meditation together, directing positive intentions and wishes towards each other, as well as towards friends, family, and even strangers. This shared practice can promote empathy, compassion, and a greater understanding of each other's emotional experiences.

4. Mindful Communication: Make a conscious effort to practice mindful communication and active listening with your partner, friends, or family members. By being fully present and engaged in conversations, you can develop deeper connections and understanding.

5. Mindful Eating: Share meals together mindfully, paying attention to the tastes, textures, and smells of the food, as well as the process of eating. This practice can enhance the enjoyment of the meal and promote gratitude for the shared experience.

6. Gratitude Practice: Cultivate a shared gratitude practice by discussing the things you're grateful for together, either on a daily or weekly basis. This practice can help to foster a positive outlook, strengthen your bond, and promote a greater appreciation for each other and your shared experiences.

7. Mindful Yoga or Exercise: Participate in mindful yoga or other forms of exercise together. By focusing on your breath, movements, and body sensations, you can develop a greater sense of connection and shared presence.

8. Mindfulness Workshops or Retreats: Attend mindfulness workshops, classes, or retreats together to deepen your practice and explore new techniques. This shared experience can help to strengthen your bond and provide a supportive environment for personal growth.

9. Compassionate Support: Offer compassionate support to each other in times of stress or emotional difficulty. By practicing empathy, understanding, and non-judgmental listening, you can create a safe space for emotional expression and healing.

10. Creating Mindful Rituals: Establish shared rituals or routines that incorporate mindfulness practices, such as starting the day with a meditation session or setting intentions for the day together. These rituals can help to create a sense of connection and shared purpose in your relationship.

Achieving Balance and Inner Peace

The Importance of Mental and Emotional Balance

Mental and emotional balance plays a crucial role in overall well-being, personal growth, and the ability to navigate life's challenges effectively. Achieving mental and emotional balance is essential for various aspects of our lives, including physical health, relationships, productivity, and personal fulfillment. Here are some reasons why mental and emotional balance is so important:

1. Physical Health: Mental and emotional balance has a direct impact on physical health. Chronic stress, anxiety, and emotional imbalances can contribute to a range of health issues, such as high blood pressure, weakened immune system, and increased risk of chronic diseases. By maintaining mental and emotional balance, you can promote better physical health and well-being.

2. Emotional Resilience: Achieving mental and emotional balance helps you develop emotional resilience, which enables you to cope with stress, setbacks, and challenges more effectively. Emotional resilience is essential for navigating life's ups and downs, allowing you to bounce back from adversity and maintain a positive outlook.

3. Improved Relationships: Mental and emotional balance can lead to healthier relationships, as it fosters emotional intelligence, empathy, and effective communication. By maintaining emotional balance, you can better understand and manage your own emotions and those of others, leading to stronger interpersonal connections.

4. Enhanced Productivity: When you're mentally and emotionally balanced, you're better equipped to focus, make decisions, and engage in creative problem-solving. This can lead to improved productivity and performance in both personal and professional aspects of your life.

5. Personal Growth: Achieving mental and emotional balance allows you to engage in self-reflection and personal growth. By understanding and managing your emotions effectively, you can identify areas for improvement, set meaningful goals, and work towards becoming the best version of yourself.

6. Greater Life Satisfaction: Mental and emotional balance contributes to an overall sense of well-being and life satisfaction. By cultivating emotional balance, you can experience greater joy, contentment, and fulfillment in various aspects of your life.

7. Stress Reduction: Maintaining mental and emotional balance can help reduce stress levels and alleviate the negative impact of stress on your mind and body. By managing stress effectively, you can prevent burnout, enhance overall well-being, and improve your quality of life.

8. Better Decision-Making: Mental and emotional balance allows you to approach decisions with a clear and balanced perspective. By managing your emotions effectively, you can make more rational, informed decisions that align with your values and goals.

In summary, mental, and emotional balance is essential for promoting overall well-being, personal growth, and the ability to navigate life's challenges effectively. By cultivating mental and emotional balance through mindfulness, meditation, and other self-care practices, you can improve various aspects of your life, including physical health, relationships, productivity, and personal fulfillment.

B. Strategies for Incorporating Mindfulness and Meditation into a Busy Life

Incorporating mindfulness and meditation into a busy life can be challenging, but with a few simple strategies, you can make these practices a part of your daily routine. Here are some tips for integrating mindfulness and meditation into your life, even when time is limited:

1. Start Small: Begin with short meditation sessions, as little as 5 to 10 minutes per day. This can help you develop a consistent practice without feeling overwhelmed by the time commitment. As you become more comfortable, you can gradually increase the duration of your sessions.

2. Prioritize Your Practice: Make mindfulness and meditation a priority by scheduling them into your daily routine. Set a specific time each day for your practice, such as first thing in the morning or before bed and treat it as an important appointment with yourself.

3. Use Reminders: Set reminders on your phone or computer to pause and practice mindfulness throughout the day. These brief moments of mindful awareness can help you cultivate presence and reduce stress.

4. Mindful Moments: Look for opportunities to practice mindfulness during everyday activities, such as washing dishes, brushing your teeth, or waiting in line. By focusing on your breath, body sensations, or surroundings, you can bring mindfulness into your daily life.

5. Mini-Meditations: When you're short on time, try mini-meditations, which are brief moments of focused attention and relaxation. These can be as simple as taking a few deep breaths, scanning your body for tension, or repeating a calming mantra.

6. Use Guided Meditation Apps: Guided meditation apps can be a helpful tool for busy individuals looking to incorporate mindfulness and meditation into their lives. These apps offer a variety of guided meditation sessions, often ranging from just a few minutes to longer sessions, making it easy to find a practice that fits your schedule.

7. Combine Meditation with Exercise: Practice mindfulness while engaging in physical activities such as walking, running, or yoga. This can help you maximize your time by combining physical exercise with mental relaxation and focus.

8. Create a Mindful Environment: Designate a space in your home or office for mindfulness and meditation. This can be as simple as a comfortable chair or cushion in a quiet corner. Having a dedicated space for your practice can help you establish a routine and reinforce the importance of mindfulness in your life.

9. Join a Meditation Group or Class: Participating in a group meditation or mindfulness class can provide accountability, support, and motivation for maintaining a consistent practice. Many communities offer classes or group meditation sessions, either in-person or online.

10. Be Patient and Persistent: Developing a consistent mindfulness and meditation practice takes time and persistence. Remember that progress may be gradual, and it's essential to be patient with yourself as you navigate the challenges of incorporating mindfulness into your busy life.

By implementing these strategies, you can successfully incorporate mindfulness and meditation into your daily routine, even with a busy schedule. Consistent practice can lead to numerous benefits, including reduced stress, improved focus, and enhanced overall well-being.

Techniques for Maintaining Inner Peace Amidst External Chaos

In today's fast-paced and often chaotic world, it can be challenging to maintain a sense of inner peace. However, with the right techniques and mindset, it is possible to cultivate and sustain inner tranquillity, even in the face of external chaos. Here are some strategies to help you maintain inner peace amidst external turmoil:

1. Mindfulness Meditation: Engage in regular mindfulness meditation practice to develop awareness and acceptance of your thoughts and emotions. By observing your inner experience without judgment, you can cultivate a sense of inner calm and equanimity.
2. Deep Breathing: When you feel overwhelmed or stressed, practice deep, slow breathing to activate your parasympathetic nervous system and promote relaxation. Focusing on your breath can help you find a sense of calm amidst the chaos.

3. Set Boundaries: Establish and maintain healthy boundaries with your time, energy, and relationships. By prioritizing self-care and setting limits on external demands, you can protect your inner peace and prevent burnout.

4. Focus on What You Can Control: Recognize that you cannot control everything in your environment and focus on the aspects of your life that you can influence. By concentrating on what you can control, you can minimize feelings of helplessness and empower yourself to take positive action.

5. Limit Exposure to Negative Influences: Be mindful of the sources of negativity in your life, such as excessive news consumption or toxic relationships. Limit your exposure to these influences and prioritize activities and interactions that promote positivity and well-being.

6. Cultivate Gratitude: Develop a daily gratitude practice to help shift your focus away from external chaos and towards the positive aspects of your life. This perspective can help you maintain a sense of inner peace, even in challenging circumstances.

7. Practice Acceptance: Accept the reality of the present moment, even when it is difficult or uncomfortable. By practicing acceptance, you can reduce resistance and suffering and foster a sense of inner peace amidst external chaos.

8. Seek Support: Connect with friends, family, or a support group to share your experiences and feelings. Seeking support can help you feel understood, validated, and less alone in your struggles.

9. Engage in Relaxation Techniques: Incorporate relaxation techniques into your daily routine, such as progressive muscle relaxation, guided imagery, or yoga. These practices can help you release tension, calm your mind, and maintain inner peace.

10. Cultivate Compassion: Practice compassion for yourself and others, recognizing that everyone faces challenges and struggles. By cultivating compassion, you can foster a sense of connection and empathy, reducing feelings of isolation and increasing inner peace.

By implementing these techniques, you can maintain inner peace amidst external chaos and navigate life's challenges with resilience and grace. Cultivating inner peace is an ongoing process that requires intention, practice, and self-compassion, but the rewards of a more peaceful and balanced life are well worth the effort.

The Importance of Mental and Emotional Balance

Mental and emotional balance plays a crucial role in overall well-being, personal growth, and the ability to navigate life's challenges effectively. Achieving mental and emotional balance is essential for various aspects of our lives, including physical health, relationships, productivity, and personal fulfillment. Here are some reasons why mental and emotional balance is so important:

1. Physical Health: Mental and emotional balance has a direct impact on physical health. Chronic stress, anxiety, and emotional imbalances can contribute to a range of health issues, such as high blood pressure, weakened immune system, and increased risk of chronic diseases. By maintaining mental and emotional balance, you can promote better physical health and well-being.

2. Emotional Resilience: Achieving mental and emotional balance helps you develop emotional resilience, which enables you to cope with stress, setbacks, and challenges more effectively. Emotional resilience is essential

for navigating life's ups and downs, allowing you to bounce back from adversity and maintain a positive outlook.

3. Improved Relationships: Mental and emotional balance can lead to healthier relationships, as it fosters emotional intelligence, empathy, and effective communication. By maintaining emotional balance, you can better understand and manage your own emotions and those of others, leading to stronger interpersonal connections.

4. Enhanced Productivity: When you're mentally and emotionally balanced, you're better equipped to focus, make decisions, and engage in creative problem-solving. This can lead to improved productivity and performance in both personal and professional aspects of your life.

5. Personal Growth: Achieving mental and emotional balance allows you to engage in self-reflection and personal growth. By understanding and managing your emotions effectively, you can identify areas for improvement, set meaningful goals, and work towards becoming the best version of yourself.

6. Greater Life Satisfaction: Mental and emotional balance contributes to an overall sense of well-being and life satisfaction. By cultivating emotional balance, you can experience greater joy, contentment, and fulfillment in various aspects of your life.

7. Stress Reduction: Maintaining mental and emotional balance can help reduce stress levels and alleviate the negative impact of stress on your mind and body. By managing stress effectively, you can prevent burnout, enhance overall well-being, and improve your quality of life.

8. Better Decision-Making: Mental and emotional balance allows you to approach decisions with a clear and balanced perspective. By managing

your emotions effectively, you can make more rational, informed decisions that align with your values and goals.

Strategies for Incorporating Mindfulness and Meditation into a Busy Life

Incorporating mindfulness and meditation into a busy life can be challenging, but with a few simple strategies, you can make these practices a part of your daily routine. Here are some tips for integrating mindfulness and meditation into your life, even when time is limited:

1. Start Small: Begin with short meditation sessions, as little as 5 to 10 minutes per day. This can help you develop a consistent practice without feeling overwhelmed by the time commitment. As you become more comfortable, you can gradually increase the duration of your sessions.
2. Prioritize Your Practice: Make mindfulness and meditation a priority by scheduling them into your daily routine. Set a specific time each day for your practice, such as first thing in the morning or before bed and treat it as an important appointment with yourself.
3. Use Reminders: Set reminders on your phone or computer to pause and practice mindfulness throughout the day. These brief moments of mindful awareness can help you cultivate presence and reduce stress.
4. Mindful Moments: Look for opportunities to practice mindfulness during everyday activities, such as washing dishes, brushing your teeth, or waiting in line. By focusing on your breath, body sensations, or surroundings, you can bring mindfulness into your daily life.
5. Mini-Meditations: When you're short on time, try mini-meditations, which are brief moments of focused attention and relaxation. These can be as simple

as taking a few deep breaths, scanning your body for tension, or repeating a calming mantra.

6. Use Guided Meditation Apps: Guided meditation apps can be a helpful tool for busy individuals looking to incorporate mindfulness and meditation into their lives. These apps offer a variety of guided meditation sessions, often ranging from just a few minutes to longer sessions, making it easy to find a practice that fits your schedule.

7. Combine Meditation with Exercise: Practice mindfulness while engaging in physical activities such as walking, running, or yoga. This can help you maximize your time by combining physical exercise with mental relaxation and focus.

8. Create a Mindful Environment: Designate a space in your home or office for mindfulness and meditation. This can be as simple as a comfortable chair or cushion in a quiet corner. Having a dedicated space for your practice can help you establish a routine and reinforce the importance of mindfulness in your life.

9. Join a Meditation Group or Class: Participating in a group meditation or mindfulness class can provide accountability, support, and motivation for maintaining a consistent practice. Many communities offer classes or group meditation sessions, either in-person or online.

10. Be Patient and Persistent: Developing a consistent mindfulness and meditation practice takes time and persistence. Remember that progress may be gradual, and it's essential to be patient with yourself as you navigate the challenges of incorporating mindfulness into your busy life.

By implementing these strategies, you can successfully incorporate mindfulness and meditation into your daily routine, even with a busy schedule. Consistent practice can lead to numerous benefits, including reduced stress, improved focus, and enhanced overall well-being.

Embracing the Magic of Mindfulness and Meditation in Everyday Life

Incorporating mindfulness and meditation into your everyday life can transform your experiences, boost your overall well-being, and help you cultivate a more balanced and fulfilling lifestyle. Here are some ways to embrace the magic of mindfulness and meditation in your daily life:

1. Cultivate Gratitude: Develop a daily gratitude practice by reflecting on the things you appreciate in your life. This can help shift your focus towards the positive aspects of your life and promote a more balanced and content mindset.

2. Practice Mindful Breathing: Make a habit of taking short mindful breathing breaks throughout the day. Focusing on your breath can help centre your thoughts, reduce stress, and bring you back to the present moment.

3. Engage Your Senses: Use your senses to experience everyday activities more fully. Pay attention to the sights, sounds, smells, tastes, and textures of your experiences, whether you're eating a meal, walking in nature, or simply sitting at your desk.

4. Develop Mindful Habits: Incorporate mindfulness into daily routines, such as making your bed, brushing your teeth, or preparing your morning coffee. By focusing on the present moment during these activities, you can train your mind to be more present throughout the day.

5. Practice Loving-Kindness: Integrate loving-kindness meditation into your daily routine to cultivate compassion and empathy for yourself and others.

This practice can help you develop more positive relationships and foster a deeper sense of connection with those around you.

6. Mindful Listening: Enhance your communication skills by practicing mindful listening. By giving your full attention to the person speaking and withholding judgment, you can develop deeper connections and understanding in your relationships.

7. Embrace Impermanence: Accept the impermanent nature of life, acknowledging that change is an inevitable part of our existence. By embracing impermanence, you can learn to adapt to change more effectively and experience a greater sense of peace and equanimity.

8. Cultivate Self-Awareness: Use mindfulness and meditation to develop a greater understanding of your thoughts, emotions, and behaviours. This self-awareness can lead to personal growth, improved emotional regulation, and enhanced decision-making abilities.

9. Practice Non-Attachment: Learn to let go of attachment to outcomes, possessions, and relationships. By practicing non-attachment, you can experience greater freedom, contentment, and inner peace.

10. Seek Balance: Use mindfulness and meditation to help you maintain a balanced lifestyle, prioritizing self-care, rest, and leisure alongside work and other responsibilities. By seeking balance, you can cultivate a more harmonious and fulfilling life experience.

By embracing the magic of mindfulness and meditation in everyday life, you can transform your daily experiences and cultivate a more balanced, fulfilling, and joyful existence. These practices can have a profound impact on your well-being, relationships, and overall quality of life, helping you navigate life's challenges with grace and resilience.

Appendix: Additional Resources

A. Recommended Books, Articles, and Podcasts on Mindfulness and Meditation

Here's a list of recommended resources to deepen your understanding of mindfulness and meditation and enhance your practice:

Books:

1. "The Miracle of Mindfulness" by Thich Nhat Hanh - This classic book by Vietnamese Zen Master Thich Nhat Hanh offers practical guidance on incorporating mindfulness into daily life and understanding its transformative power.
2. "Wherever You Go, There You Are" by Jon Kabat-Zinn - A foundational book on mindfulness, written by the creator of the Mindfulness-Based Stress Reduction (MBSR) program. It provides insights and exercises to help you develop a consistent mindfulness practice.
3. "The Power of Now" by Eckhart Tolle - This best-selling book explores the concept of living in the present moment, offering practical advice on overcoming negative thought patterns and cultivating inner peace.
4. "Radical Acceptance" by Tara Brach - This book combines mindfulness and self-compassion practices with insights from Buddhist psychology, providing guidance on how to embrace your imperfections and develop greater self-acceptance.

5. "Mindfulness in Plain English" by Bhante Gunaratana - A clear and concise guide to mindfulness meditation, offering practical instructions and advice for developing a consistent meditation practice.

Articles

1. "Mindfulness: Getting Started" by mindful.org - This article provides a beginner's guide to mindfulness, including simple practices to incorporate into daily life: https://www.mindful.org/mindfulness-how-to-do-it/

2. "7 Ways Meditation Can Actually Change The Brain" by Alice G. Walton - This Forbes article discusses the scientific research on the neurological benefits of meditation: https://www.forbes.com/sites/alicegwalton/2015/02/09/7-ways-meditation-can-actually-change-the-brain/

3. "The Science of Mindfulness: A Research-Based Path to Well-Being" by Ronald D. Siegel - This article discusses the science behind mindfulness and its applications for well-being: https://www.apa.org/monitor/2012/07-08/ce-corner

1. The Daily Meditation Podcast - Hosted by Mary Meckley, this podcast offers daily guided meditations and mindfulness techniques to reduce stress and enhance well-being. (https://thedailymeditationpodcast.libsyn.com/)

2. The Mindful Minute - Hosted by Meryl Arnett, The Mindful Minute offers guided meditations, mindfulness teachings, and interviews with experts to help deepen your practice. (https://merylarnett.com/the-mindful-minute/)

3. Ten Percent Happier with Dan Harris - This podcast, hosted by ABC News correspondent Dan Harris, features interviews with prominent mindfulness and meditation experts, as well as guided meditation sessions. (https://www.tenpercent.com/podcast)

4. The Tara Brach Podcast - Tara Brach, a renowned meditation teacher and psychologist, shares her insights on mindfulness, self-compassion, and spiritual awakening through her podcast. (https://www.tarabrach.com/podcast/)

These books, articles, and podcasts offer valuable insights and guidance on mindfulness and meditation, helping you deepen your understanding and practice. By engaging with these resources, you can enhance your well-being, cultivate inner peace, and navigate life's challenges with greater resilience.

Workshops, retreats, and training programs for further exploration

Here is a list of a few workshops, retreats, and training programs from around the world that can help you further explore mindfulness and meditation:

Australia:

1. The Gawler Cancer Foundation - Offers various mindfulness and meditation retreats and workshops, including Mindfulness-Based Stillness Meditation (MBSM) programs. (https://gawler.org/)
2. The Art of Living Australia - Provides workshops, retreats, and courses on mindfulness, meditation, and personal development, including the popular Happiness Program. (https://www.artofliving.org/au-en)
3. Open ground - Offers Mindfulness-Based Stress Reduction (MBSR) courses and workshops in various cities across Australia. (https://www.openground.com.au/)

4. Sydney Meditation Centre - Provides various meditation and mindfulness courses, workshops, and retreats, including beginner courses and advanced training. (https://www.sydneymeditationcentre.com/)

USA:

1. Spirit Rock Meditation Centre (California) - Offers various mindfulness and meditation workshops, retreats, and training programs, including courses led by renowned teachers such as Jack Kornfield and Tara Brach. (https://www.spiritrock.org/)
2. Insight Meditation Society (Massachusetts) - Provides a range of meditation and mindfulness retreats, workshops, and courses, including residential retreats and online programs. (https://www.dharma.org/)
3. Shambhala Mountain Centre (Colorado) - Offers various mindfulness, meditation, and personal growth workshops and retreats in a serene mountain setting. (https://www.shambhalamountain.org/)
4. Omega Institute (New York) - Provides a wide variety of workshops, retreats, and training programs on mindfulness, meditation, and personal development. (https://www.eomega.org/)
5. Mindful Schools (Online) - Offers online mindfulness training programs and resources for educators, parents, and professionals, with a focus on integrating mindfulness into educational settings. (https://www.mindfulschools.org/)

These workshops, retreats, and training programs provide opportunities for immersive learning experiences in mindfulness and meditation, allowing you to deepen your practice, enhance your well-being, and connect with like-minded individuals.

Asia

1. Tushita Meditation Centre (India) - Offers introductory meditation courses, advanced meditation retreats, and special programs in the Tibetan Buddhist tradition. (https://tushita.info/)
2. Wat Suan Mokkh (Thailand) - Offers 10-day silent meditation retreats in the Buddhist tradition, focusing on mindfulness and loving-kindness practices. (https://www.suanmokkh-idh.org/)
3. Plum Village (Vietnam) - Founded by Zen Master Thich Nhat Hanh, Plum Village offers mindfulness retreats, workshops, and training programs in the tradition of Engaged Buddhism. (https://plumvillage.org/)

Europe:

1. Gaia House (UK) - Offers silent meditation retreats in the Insight Meditation tradition, featuring renowned meditation teachers from around the world. (https://gaiahouse.co.uk/)
2. Sharpham Trust (UK) - Provides a range of mindfulness and meditation retreats, workshops, and courses in a beautiful, natural setting. (https://www.sharphamtrust.org/)
3. Vipassana Meditation (Europe) - Offers 10-day silent Vipassana meditation retreats in various locations throughout Europe, following the teachings of S.N. Goenka. (https://www.dhamma.org/en/index)

Netherlands:

1. Amsterdam Insight Meditation - Offers Mindfulness-Based Stress Reduction (MBSR) courses, workshops, and retreats, as well as insight meditation retreats and courses. (https://amsterdam.insightmeditation.nl/)
2. Centrum voor Mindfulness (CVM) - Provides a range of mindfulness courses, workshops, and training programs, including MBSR/MBCT teacher training and courses for professionals. (https://centrumvoormindfulness.nl/)
3. Maitri Retreats (Netherlands) - Offers mindfulness and loving-kindness meditation retreats, workshops, and courses in various locations in the Netherlands. (https://maitriretreats.nl/)

These workshops, retreats, and training programs provide opportunities for immersive learning experiences in mindfulness and meditation, allowing you to deepen your practice, enhance your well-being, and connect with like-minded individuals across different countries and cultural contexts

VI. Summary

Recap of key takeaways from the book

1. Positive thinking is a powerful tool that can help you overcome obstacles, cultivate resilience, and achieve your goals.
2. Negative thoughts and self-limiting beliefs can be insidious and sabotage our efforts to grow and thrive. We must learn to identify them and challenge their validity.
3. Reframing negative thoughts into more positive, realistic ones is an effective strategy for promoting mental and physical well-being.

4. Practicing gratitude, surrounding ourselves with positivity, and engaging in activities that bring us joy and fulfillment can all contribute to a more positive mindset.
5. Embracing a growth mindset, learning from setbacks, and maintaining perspective during times of change and uncertainty are essential for personal growth and development.
6. Self-compassion and forgiveness are crucial for maintaining a positive outlook and nurturing healthy relationships.
7. Positive thinking can have a transformative impact on our lives, but it requires consistent effort and practice.

By embracing these key principles and strategies, you can cultivate a positive mindset and unlock your full potential. Remember to be patient and kind to yourself throughout your journey and celebrate each step of progress along the way.

Reflection on personal growth and the power of positive thinking

As we come to the end of our journey through Mindshift Magic, it's important to take a moment to reflect on the transformative power of positive thinking and personal growth. By embracing a positive mindset and practicing the strategies outlined in this book, you have the power to shape your destiny and create a life of limitless potential.

Throughout the book, we've explored the science behind positive thinking, the importance of self-compassion and forgiveness, strategies for reframing negative thoughts, and ways to create a supportive environment. We've also delved into how positive thinking can improve relationships, maintain a positive mindset during times of change and uncertainty, and more.

By putting these concepts into practice, you have the ability to overcome obstacles, achieve your goals, and cultivate a sense of inner peace and fulfillment. But remember, personal growth is a lifelong journey, and it's important to continue to explore and cultivate your mindset and practices as you move forward.

As you move forward on your journey, I encourage you to remain open to new experiences and possibilities, to practice self-compassion and forgiveness, and to surround yourself with positivity. Remember that setbacks and challenges are opportunities for growth and embrace the power of a growth mindset to help you navigate uncertainty and change.

Finally, I want to express my gratitude to you for taking the time to read this book and explore the world of positive thinking and personal growth. It's my hope that you have gained valuable insights and tools to help you unleash your limitless potential and create the life you've always envisioned. So go forth and embrace the magic of positive thinking, knowing that the power to shape your destiny lies within you.

Call to action for readers to continue their journey towards a limitless life through positive thinking

As we come to the end of this book, I want to leave you with a final call to action. Throughout the pages of this book, we've explored the transformative power of positive thinking, and how it can help you overcome obstacles, cultivate meaningful relationships, and achieve your goals. But it's not enough to simply read about these concepts - to truly embrace a positive mindset and unlock your limitless potential, you must put them into practice in your daily life.

So, my challenge to you is this: take what you've learned from this book and make a commitment to apply it in your life. Start by identifying your negative thought patterns and reframing them into more positive, constructive perspectives. Cultivate gratitude, seek out positivity, and surround yourself with supportive individuals who share your values and goals. Embrace the unknown and maintain perspective during times of change and uncertainty. And most importantly, continue to nurture a growth mindset, seeking out opportunities for learning and personal development.

Remember, the journey towards a limitless life is a lifelong endeavour. It requires dedication, effort, and a willingness to challenge yourself and step outside of your comfort zone. But with the tools, strategies, and insights you've gained from this book, I have no doubt that you're capable of achieving great things.

So, go forth and unleash the magic of positive thinking in your life, and may you discover the infinite potential that lies within you.